SENIORS GUIDE TO
Windows 11

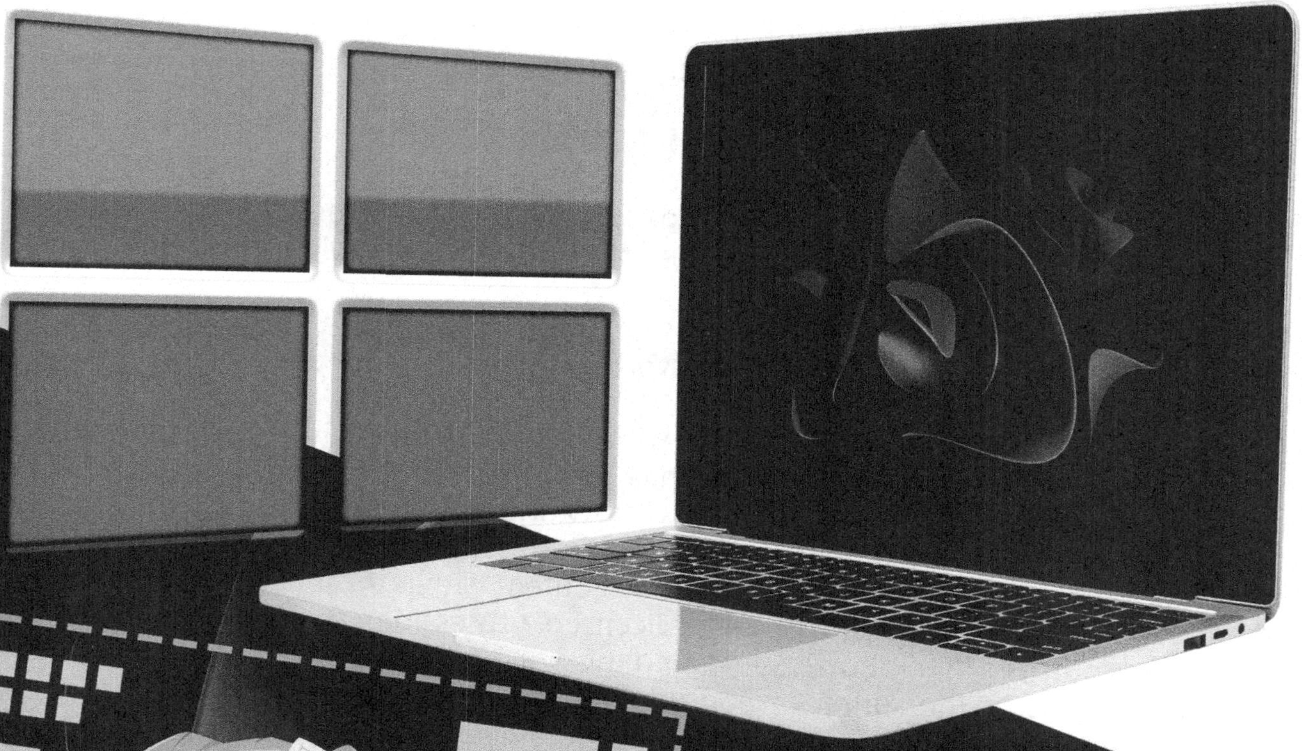

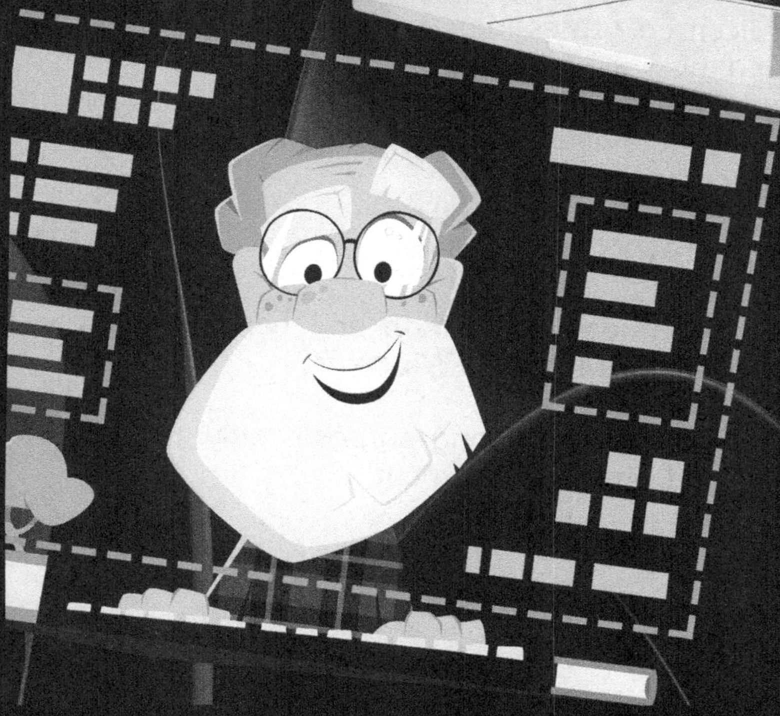

The Most Complete and Intuitive **Step-by-Step Manual** to Master **Windows 11**, with Tips and Tricks **for Senior Beginner Users**

TABLE OF CONTENTS

21°C
Sunny intervals

12:00 AM
01/01/2022

CHAPTER 5: HOW TO NAVIGATE ON THE WEB WITH WINDOWS 11 78

CHAPTER 6: EMAILING WITH FAMILY AND FRIENDS 90

CHAPTER 7: CONNECTING WITH MICROSOFT TEAMS 101

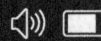

21°C
Sunny intervals

12:00 AM
01/01/2022

CHAPTER 10: HAVING FUN WITH WINDOWS 11 135

CHAPTER 11: TIPS AND TRICKS 146

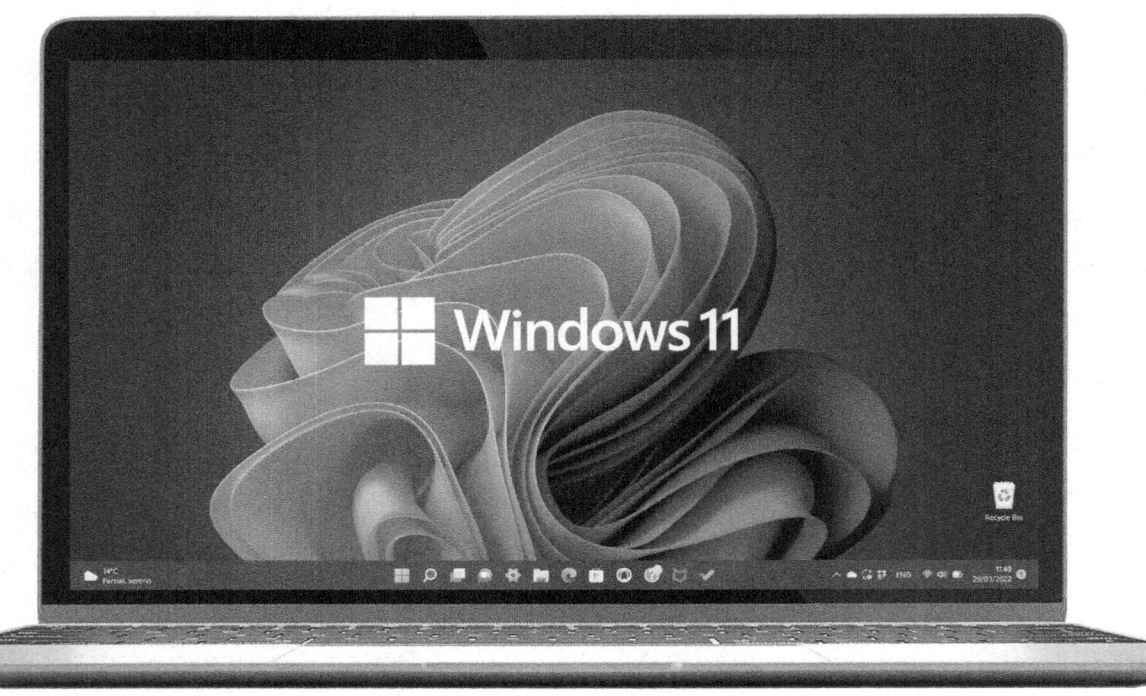

GLOSSARY

APPLICATION - code installed into your computer that performs specific tasks or functions. They are also known as programs or software.

BROWSER - an application used to access and navigate the internet, such as Google Chrome, Microsoft Edge, or Firefox.

CPU - "central processing unit," the unit that works as the 'brain' of the computer, carrying out arithmetic and logic calculations.

CRASH - when a piece of software or hardware malfunctions.

CURSOR - the arrow on screen connected to your mouse that is used to carry out actions by clicking.

DEFAULT - the settings or programs that come standard with your computer.

DESKTOP - the main directory or working area of your computer that you use to access other directories and applications.

DISK - the storage device installed into your computer.

DOWNLOAD - transferring data, such as programs, photos, files and documents, or other media, from the internet into your computer.

EMAIL - "electronic mail," a digital message that can be sent using the internet.

HARDWARE - physical and mechanical components that are installed into your computer such as hard drives, chips, keyboards, monitors, etc.

ICONS - pictures that represent links to a program or function on your computer.

INPUT DEVICE - the hardware you use to interact with your computer, such as mouse, keyboard, microphone, etc.

INSTALL - preparing and making software or hardware ready for use.

INTERFACE - a device like a monitor, or a program like a desktop, that enables you to communicate with your computer.

INTERNET - interconnected computer networks.

MEMORY - information that is stored on your computer.

MENU - a list of options that can carry out different functions. Can include pop-up menus, drop-down menus, and more.

MONITOR - the screen or visual display connected to your computer.

MOUSE - hardware that you move about with your hand to control the on-screen cursor and click buttons.

MP3 - a file format used to store video and audio data.

MULTIMEDIA - any kind of media, including audio and video.

NETWORK - a system of interconnected computers.

OPERATING SYSTEM - Software that manages all other software and hardware on your computer, laptop, or tablet, ensuring that all files, programs, and processes can access the hard drives, processing units, memory, and storage efficiently and adequately.

PLUG AND PLAY - hardware that can be plugged in and are instantly recognized by the computer allowing them to be used right away, like a mouse, keyboard, hard drive, etc.

PROGRAM - same as application.

RAM - 'random access memory' is storage in your computer used to help run background processes for different programs, helping them run faster.

VIRUS - a code that can copy itself and cause damage to your computer or threaten your computer security. Malware is similar.

WEBCAM - a digital camera that connects to your computer and can send live footage to the internet.

WINDOW - a section of your display that is used to show the graphics of a program.

WORD PROCESSOR - a program used to create, edit, and save documents.

INTRODUCTION

GETTING TO KNOW WINDOWS 11

WHAT IS WINDOWS 11?

Windows 11 is the latest version of Microsoft's Windows operating system. An operating system manages all software and hardware on your computer, laptop, or tablet, ensuring that all files, programs, and processes can access the hard drives, processing units, memory, and storage efficiently and adequately.

There have been several different versions of Windows released over the years. **Windows 1 was released in 1985**, evolving into more modern versions such as Windows 95,

WindowsXP, Windows 7, Windows 8, Windows 10, and the most recent version, which we will learn about in this book. Each version has seen updates and changes to how the operating system looks and feels and more technical changes that run in the background to make your experience with your computer more intuitive and efficient.

There are other operating systems that can run on computers such as Linux, Ubuntu, Android, ChromeOS, and macOS. Each of these operating systems is designed to meet the specific needs of different users. Some are better for carrying out office tasks like writing documents and emails, while others write code and develop software.

Operating systems are also designed for different kinds of devices; for example, smartphones use Android or IOS, which are made for mobile devices and suited for running small apps, whereas computers need more comprehensive operating systems with many different pieces of hardware and software.

Windows 11, like other types of operating systems, presents you with a graphical user interface. This is a way of allowing you to communicate with your computer system, your mouse, or touchscreen by clicking on different symbols or icons. Before graphical user interfaces were the norm, character user interfaces were used. In a character user interface or command-line interface, you would have to write specific lines of code orcommands in order to carry out different tasks and functions.

WHY USE WINDOWS?

Windows is one of the most common operating systems available on the market, coming standard with most PCs and laptops except for Apple products. Its advantages over its alternatives include its ease of use, extensive range of compatible software, backward compatibility, hardware support, plug and play, and gaming features.

Microsoft Windows is easy to use because it has a standardized design with features to help teach and guide the user through the many different features offered. The operating system is compatible with most programs and software you may wish to use, from business and accounting software to music and media apps and even games. Software developers are forced to ensure their programs work with Windows, or they will lose out on a large majority of the sales market. Windows offers backward compatibility, which simply means that if you are using older versions of a program, it will almost always run on the most recent versions of Windows even if it was installed on a much older version. It helps protect the user from losing important information or games when they upgrade the operating system.

_ ☐ ✕

Due to Microsoft Windows' dominance in the market, software and hardware manufacturers must ensure that their components are compatible with the operating system. Most hardware components, ranging from hard drives, motherboards, graphics cards, processing units, fans, mouses, keyboards, webcams, and power supplies, will work with the Windows operating system immediately without configuring. This is known as plug-and-play. Finally, most computer games are developed to be used with Windows operating systems. Windows offers hardware support for all the various requirements that a game may require and can help to optimize the way the game runs, so you do not have to deal with glitches or slowness.

Of course, Microsoft Windows has some disadvantages compared to other operating systems available on the market. Due to all the features offered in the operating system, it requires a lot of resources and suitable hardware. The central processing unit (CPU), hard disk, and memory drives will become overloaded if they cannot manage all of the processes necessary to run Windows, which can rack up the costs.

Windows is a closed source operating system, which means that the code is proprietary and cannot be altered or changed by the user. This is compared to open-source operating systems, such as Linux or Ubuntu, where the user can easily make changes to the code to customize different functions or processes to suit their specific needs. This can be a limiting factor for people that work in highly technical fields like software development or internet security. Still, it is not really an important factor for the average computer user. Windows also have strict licensing agreements, requiring users to ensure their computers are kept up to date or certain features will not work correctly and can involve expensive subscription plans.

HOW WINDOWS HAS EVOLVED OVER TIME

Let's take a quick look at some of the ways that the Windows operating system has evolved and changed so that you can fully appreciate the features offered in the newest version.

Windows 1 was the very first version to be released by Microsoft, and it offered a very simple graphical user interface where a mouse could control a cursor on the screen.

Windows 2 followed a few years later and introduced the ability to 16 color graphic displays. These displays produced different information windows that could be minimized and maximized. Windows 2 also introduced keyboard shortcuts and the earliest versions of the office programs MS Word and MS Excel.

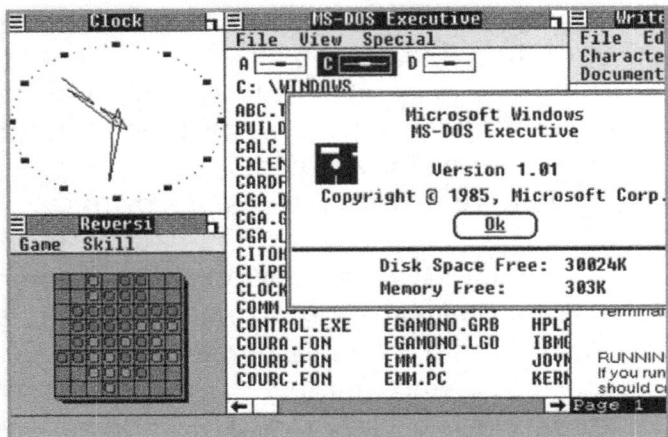

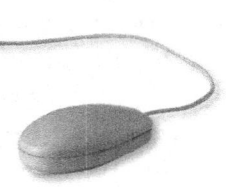

Windows 1

Windows 3 was the first version to be released on a CD-ROM. It saw the release of various managers that supported the user in carrying out different tasks rather than relying on command-line prompts or lines of code. Some of these managers are still used in modern versions and include the File Manager, Control Panel, Print Manager, and Program Manager. Windows 3 introduced 256 colors allowing the interface to be modernized and customized and significantly included networking features allowing connections to be established between multiple different computers.

Windows 95 is one of the earliest versions that begins to resemble the modern versions of the operating system, with the Taskbar spanning the bottom of the screen and its Start Menu in the left-hand corner. Windows 95 offered dial-up support for connecting to the internet and the first Internet Explorer browser. It also provided multimedia features such as the automatic configuration of different pieces of hardware used for multimedia, applications for working with video, sound, graphics, and images, and video support with higher frame rates and quicker processing speeds.

21°C
Sunny intervals

12:00 AM
01/01/2022

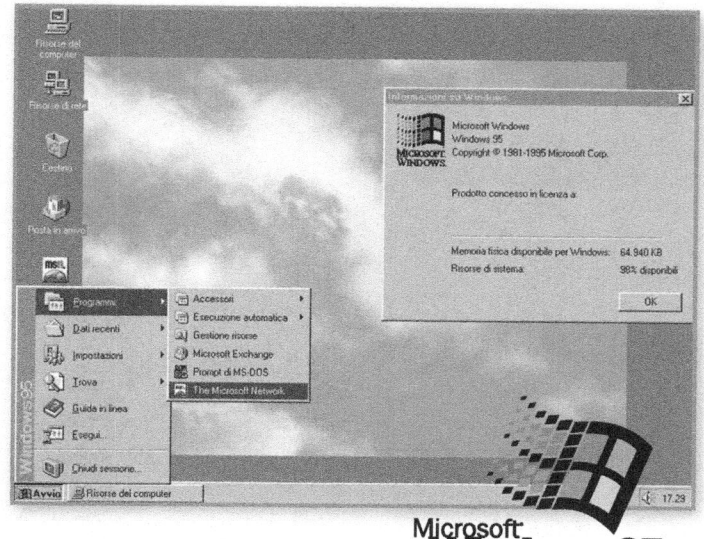

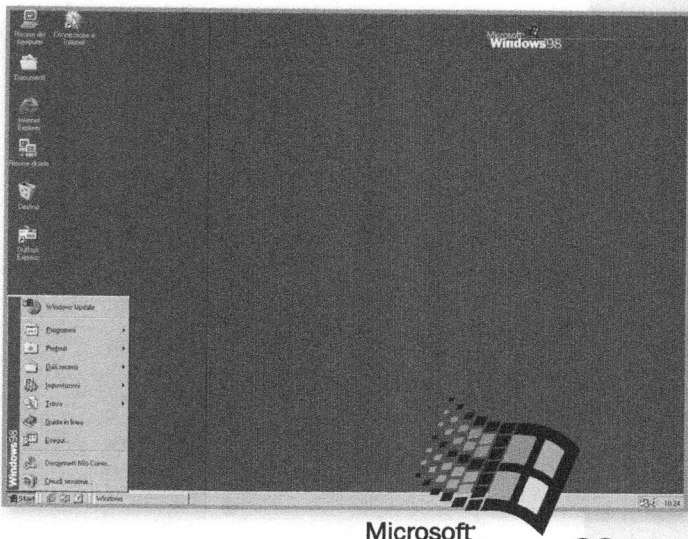

As the versions were updated, their demand for resources also increased. **Windows 98, released in 1998, needed more memory and storage space than previous versions**, and many computers did not come standard with this hardware, requiring the user to go out and purchase the necessary upgrades. However, this was a small price to pay for the additional features and functionality on offer. **Windows 98 supported not only CD-ROMS but also DVD and USB.** Additional features were added to manage background processes, such as an update manager, internet sharing manager, and disk cleanup.

Windows 2000 was released in the hopes that it would be adopted for many business purposes, offering unique business solutions such as file encryption to keep data safe and secure, and server capabilities.

Windows XP was by far one of Microsoft's biggest successes, selling over 17 million licensed copies in the two months after its release date (*Microsoft, 2002*). Compared to Windows 2000, which was marketed towards business solutions, Windows XP was crafted and designed for the average home user. It featured an overhauled appearance with transparent windows, drop shadows, and customizable visual styles. The Start menu was altered and updated to feature a two-column layout showing all the applications installed on the computer and frequently used programs and documents. A firewall to help protect the computer from internet traffic and the ability to burn CDs were also introduced in this version.

Microsoft
Windows 2000

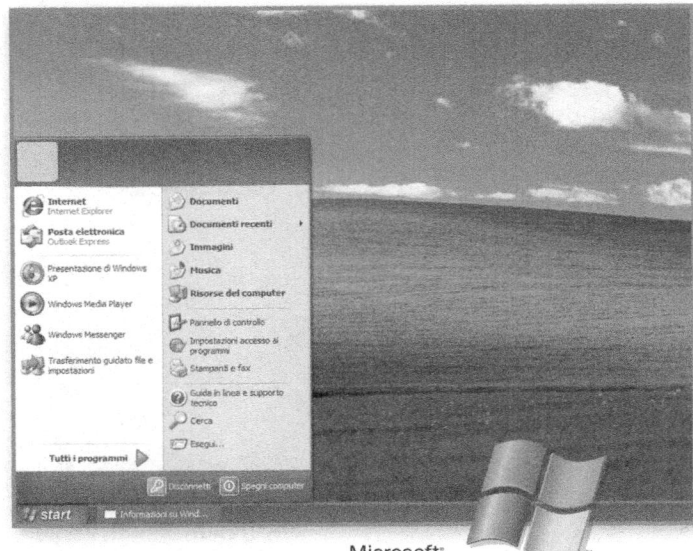

Microsoft
Windows xp

_ □ ✕

Windows Vista was one of Microsoft's least successful versions, struggling to compete with the major success of Windows XP. It improved some aspects of graphics display and memory management and had much higher hardware requirements, making it inefficient and prone to bugs. Windows Vista would no longer support many programs compatible with Windows XP, and there were other general changes to the interface's appearance that consumers did not like.

Windows 7 was released in 2009 and was developed better to meet the needs of wireless devices such as laptops. It featured touch, speech, and handwriting recognition, making it easier for people with various disabilities to use, supporting a more extensive range of different file formats. Once again, the taskbar was upgraded and decluttered, making it run more efficiently and offering the user a more streamlined experience. The file manager was improved and optimized, and the hardware requirements were not much larger than that of the previous versions. Many users jumped straight from Windows XP to Windows 7, skipping Windows Vista entirely.

Windows 8 was a great risk as Microsoft endeavored to take advantage of the touch screens offered by many mobile devices, including laptops, tablets, and smartphones. This version did not do very well and was short-lived but saw changes such as a completely overhauled interface with a tile-type start menu, with the start button being removed

21°C
Sunny intervals

12:00 AM
01/01/2022

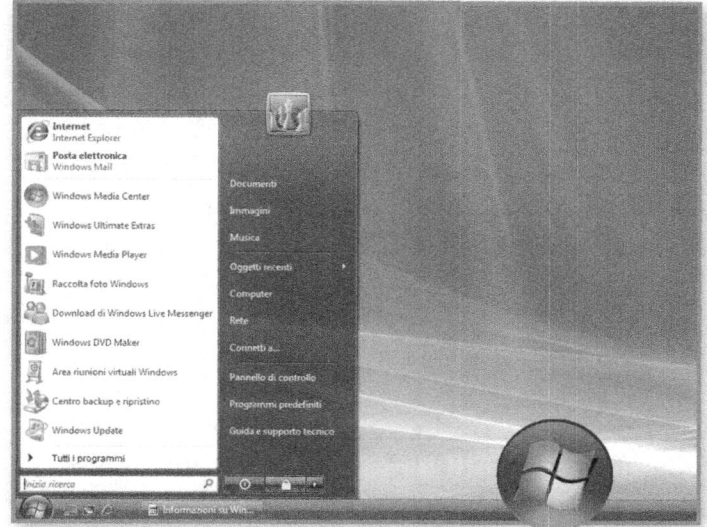

Windows Vista™

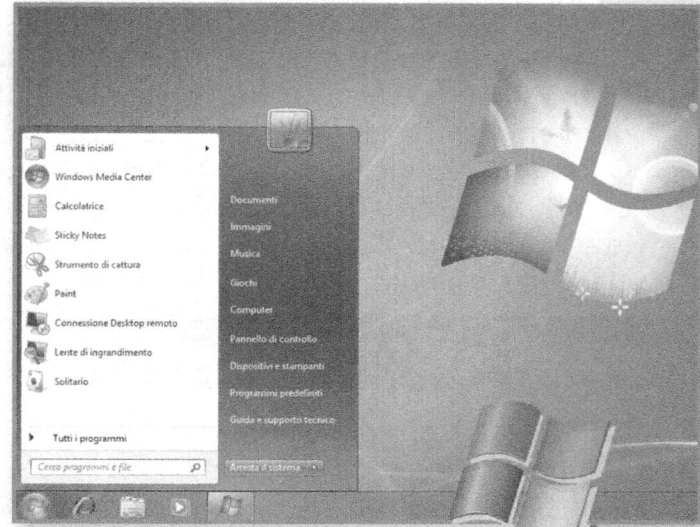

Windows 7™

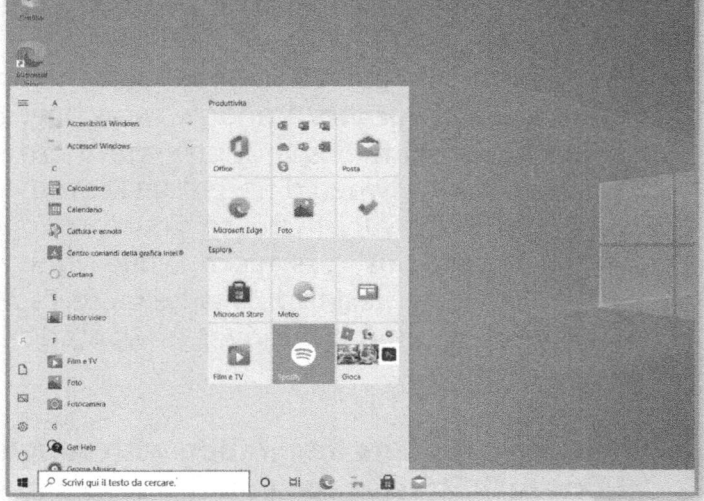

Windows 8™

Windows 10

completely. This version had quicker start-up times, but many users that had gotten so used to the previous layout and interfaces found it challenging to adjust to such drastic changes.

21°C
Sunny intervals

12:00 AM
01/01/2022

_ □ ✕

Windows 10 (yes, there was no version 9) **saw a return to the more traditional desktop as the tile interface was done away with.** It supports universal apps that work on many different devices, including Photos, Videos, Music, Mail, Calendar, and Messaging apps. Other features include touch-based and mouse-based interfaces, a new internet browser called Microsoft Edge, a newly designed Start menu, and Cortana integration. Cortana is a voice-controlled digital assistant that can help solve problems and carry out tasks without clicking or using the keyboard.

KEY FEATURES OF WINDOWS 11

Windows 11 offers several new, key features not available in previous versions. An overhaul of the look and feel or the interface is often described as more Mac-like. One of the most noticeable changes in the Task Bar, which is still located at the bottom of the display, but unlike most previous versions, the Start Menu and other application icons are now centered rather than aligned on the left-hand side. The taskbar can be customized to display only the icons you want to see, such as a list of the most recently accessed files, a search bar, or your favorite applications and programs.

A more pastel-colored palette has been adopted, and the windows now have rounded and softened corners. Windows now have new snap controls that allow you to maximize or minimize windows and arrange them side by side, in a neat grid or in groups to easily switch between different tasks. You can also set up multiple virtual desktops which can help to greatly increase your productivity. You can set up a desktop specifically for work and business tasks, while your entertainment and media can be integrated into a separate desktop. This helps to reduce the amount of distractions while you are busy working, and it removes unwanted reminders of work while you are enjoying your entertainment.

Windows 11 offers integration with various Android apps that can be accessed via the Microsoft Store 📱 **or Amazon Appstore.** This means that you can use many of your favorite smartphone apps on your computer, including WhatsApp, helping to create a seamless transition as you switch between different devices.

Widgets are another new feature that you can take advantage of in Windows 11. Though they have been introduced in previous versions, the developers have worked hard to smoothly integrate widgets into the desktop without interfering with other functions or reducing performance.

A widget is a small app that can display dynamic information on your desktop without

21°C
Sunny intervals

12:00 AM
01/01/2022

 Windows 11

you needing to open and start up the app. Depending on your needs, they can be moved, rearranged, resized, and customized.

Some of the most useful widgets include Calendar, allowing you to see upcoming events, schedule appointments, or plan your daily tasks at a glance; Entertainment which shows you current information on all your favorite shows, movies, and music; Sports, alerting you to the latest scores and sporting moments to keep you up to date; Tips, offering you useful tricks and tips to optimize your computer experience; and Traffic, helping you plan your routes to and from work or the store with built-in intuitive functions that can predict what time you are expected to leave home. There are many widgets for you to choose from, customize and experiment with.

Another helpful feature that improves connectivity between you and your loved ones is built-in integration with Microsoft Teams. The application is not pinned directly to the taskbar, making it easier to use and access. You can quickly jump into a video call with friends and family.

Windows 11 has adopted some of the ease of use seen in smartphones and tablets by offering you the option of changing crucial settings simply by tapping or clicking on the sides of the taskbar. You can easily change the brightness, volume, night mode, and access connectivity controls in this way rather than having to open the Control Panel. The voice typing function has also undergone an update, improving accessibility for blind people and those with other types of vision impairments.

For users interested in playing games on their computer, Windows 11 now allows you to play Xbox One games directly on your PC. You can do this either by purchasing, downloading, and installing games on your PC or streaming directly from your Xbox console to your PC. These changes include some updates to how gaming data is stored, using the graphics cards instead, making it much faster and more efficient to load up and play various games.

There are several security updates in Windows 11 to take advantage of. Windows 11 works with specialized silicon chips that are tamper-resistant and designed to store and protect encrypted data. This is useful for people who use their computers for important and confidential business data. Windows 11 offers a few different ways to sign into your devices through the Windows Hello system. You can now use facial recognition with your laptop or tablet's camera, use fingerprint recognition if your device has a fingerprint scanner, or you can sign in using your secure PIN code. Windows Hello reduces the hassle of authenticating and verifying many of your Microsoft-linked accounts.

WHAT HAS BEEN REMOVED IN WINDOWS 11?

It is unsurprising that many features present in previous versions of Windows have been removed. This is because the functions have been replaced or integrated into newer and more modern apps, or market research has shown that they are not popular or in demand by most users.

One of the things you may miss in Windows 11 include a moveable taskbar. In previous versions, the taskbar could be moved and adjusted to lie on the sides of the screen or the top of the screen rather than the bottom. In Windows 11, the taskbar is now locked in place. The taskbar menu has also been removed, so right-clicking on the taskbar will now only bring up the taskbar settings rather than all the options available in Windows 10.

The taskbar menu(*see image on the right*) brought up when right-clicking in Windows 10 has now been removed and replaced with only taskbar settings.

Microsoft has also removed the ability to drag and drop files onto the app icons in the taskbar, which would previously open them on those apps.

— □ ✕

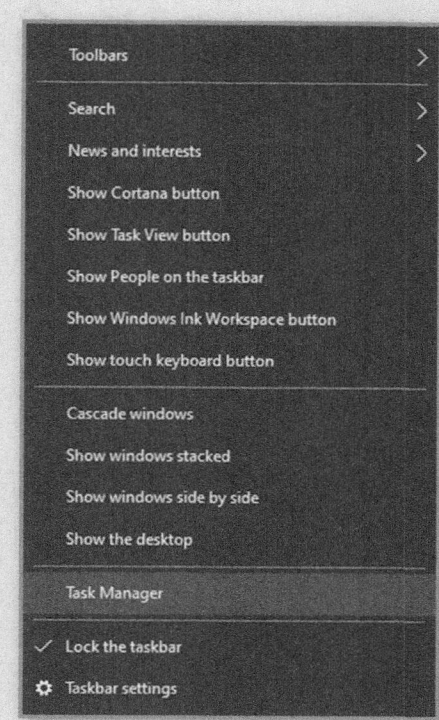

Replaced in Windows 11

Though the Calendar remains mostly unchanged, Windows 10 offered the ability to see a list of scheduled events below the calendar fly-out which appeared when you clicked on the date/time in the systems tray in the right side of the taskbar. In Windows 11 you can only see the calendar and not events, and this feature has been replaced by calendar and appointment widgets.

You will also notice some major changes to the layout of the Start menu, which now features a "Pinned apps" section with app icons, and a "Recommended apps" section showing some of the most recently or commonly used apps and files. Below these sections are the user profiles and a power button. In the previous version you could access account and user settings, the File Explorer, the Pictures app, power settings, as well as a list of apps with the most recently used icons shown at the top of the list and a section with live tiles showing app suggestions.

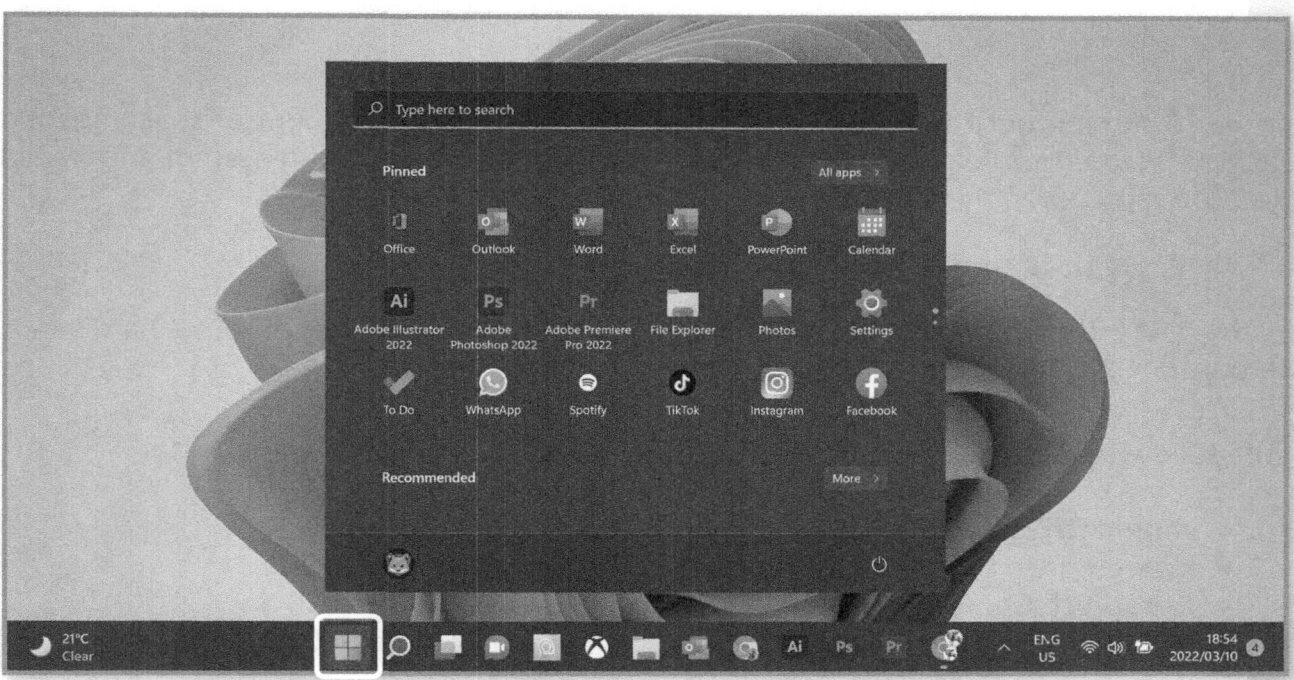

Start Menu

_ □ ✕

CAN MY COMPUTER RUN WINDOWS 11?

Like many of its predecessors, the latest iteration of Windows will require more resources and upgraded hardware to run properly. Most computers and laptops that are currently operating on Windows 10 may be eligible for Windows 11 when the operating system is rolled out between early and mid-2022. However many older models may not be eligible for this download. **Here are some of the hardware requirements that are needed to run Windows 11 properly:**

- **An internet connection** - if you are looking to upgrade to Windows 11 you will need access to the internet to download the operating system. However, many devices will soon be sold and rolled out with Windows 11 already preinstalled.

- **TPM Transfer module** - this is related to some of the security updates mentioned previously and is a requirement for Windows 11's security features. Most new devices will come with this tamper-proof silicon chip that helps with encryption services.

- **A 1Ghz or faster 64-bit processor.** You can find this information in the "Device Specifications" menu in the Settings app and it will also be clearly displayed when buying a new device. The exact meaning behind this information is not important.

- **At least 4GB of RAM**. Similar to the processor, you can also find out how much RAM is installed in your computer in the "Device Specifications" menu within the Settings app.

- **A minimum of 64GB of on-device storage.** This is the amount of space needed in your PC to download and install all of the data for the operating system and it also includes any potential space that may be required for future updates.

- **A graphics card compatible with DirectX 12.**

- **UEFI firmware** works to connect the operating system with the hardware's programming.

The following CPUs (central processing units) will be able to run Windows 11:

- **Intel 8th Gen (Coffee Lake)**
- **Intel 9th Gen (Coffee Lake Refresh)**
- **Intel 10th Gen (Comet Lake)**
- **Intel 10th Gen (Ice Lake)**

- **AMD Ryzen 2000**
- **AMD Ryzen 3000**
- **AMD Ryzen 4000**
- **AMD Ryzen 5000**

21°C
Sunny intervals

12:00 AM
01/01/2022

- **Intel 11th Gen (Rocket Lake)**
- **Intel 11th Gen (Tiger Lake)**
- **Intel 12th Gen (Alder Lake)**
- **Intel Xeon Skylake-SP**
- **Intel Xeon Cascade Lake-SP**
- **Intel Xeon Cooper Lake-SP**
- **Intel Xeon Ice Lake-SP**
- **Intel Core X-series**
- **Intel Xeon® W-series**
- **Intel Core 7820HQ**

- **AMD Ryzen 6000**
- **AMD Ryzen Threadripper 2000**
- **AMD Ryzen Threadripper 3000**
- **AMD Ryzen Threadripper Pro 3000**
- **AMD EPYC 2nd Gen**
- **AMD EPYC 3rd Gen**

This list includes most of the processors that can currently run Windows 10.

HOW TO UPGRADE WINDOWS 11

If your device is eligible for Windows 11, Microsoft will send you a notification to let you know that an upgrade is available. You can find out whether or not there is an upgrade in **SETTINGS > UPDATE & SECURITY > WINDOWS UPDATE.** Click on Check for Updates. If you are eligible, you will see the Feature update to Windows 11. Select Download and install. Then you will need to follow all the prompts as Windows carries out the installation process which can take a few minutes.

Once you have Windows 11 installed, you should regularly check for any further updates to keep your computer running optimally. You can find these updates in the same location, though Windows will also make sure to give you a notification about these downloads.

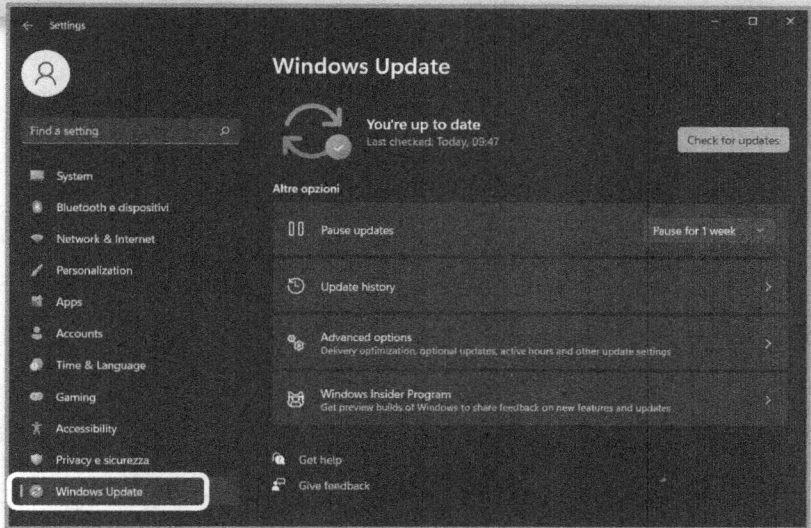

CHAPTER 1:

NAVIGATING WITH THE WINDOWS FILE EXPLORER

The primary method of navigating through the content on a Windows 11 computer is to use the File Explorer. This is a file management system and browser used to locate, manage, and delete all of your files, photos, documents, and more.

🔍 FILE EXPLORER

File Explorer was first introduced in Windows 95 and has been included in every version since, including the latest Windows 11. It is a browser that is used to navigate through the drives, libraries, folders and files on your computer. It can be used to search for documents, sort and manage different files, and offers a range of different actions to

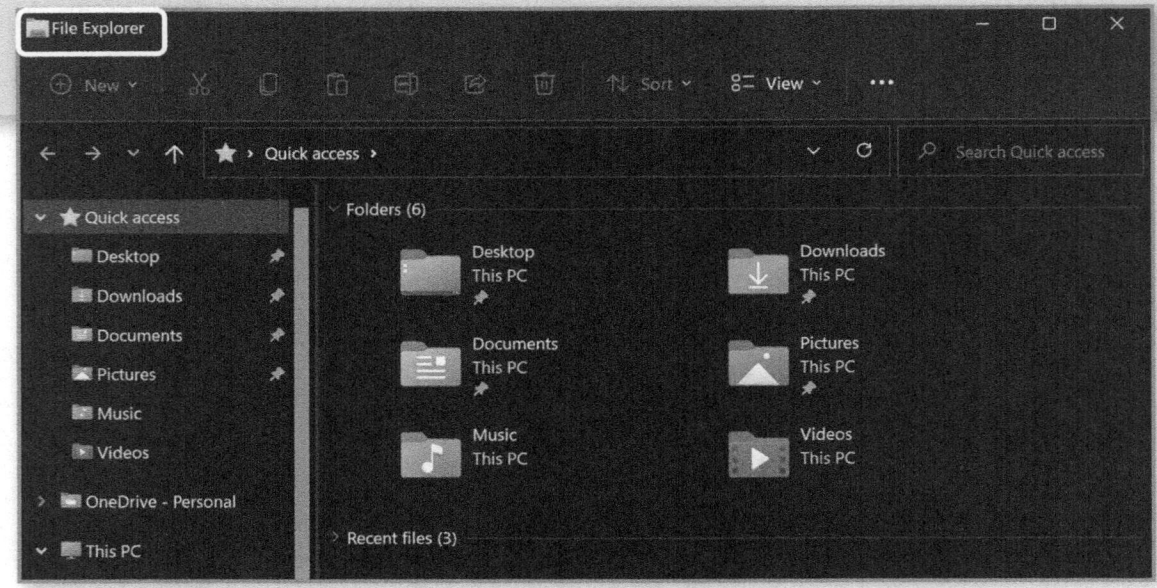

_ □ ✕

help curate your computer's library.

File explorer has undergone a makeover similar to the rest of the operating system, and many of the icons used for standard folders such as the Desktop, Documents, Downloads, Music, Pictures, Videos and disk drives may look different than what you are used to. However, the designs are still intuitive, and the colors help bring some vibrancy to your File Explorer.

HOW TO OPEN FILE EXPLORER

- **Use the keyboard shortcut Win+E** (The Win key looks like the Windows 4-panel logo) to quickly open File Explorer.

- **Click the File Explorer icon** 📁 **found in the taskbar**

- **Type "File Explorer" into the Start menu** ⊞.

NAVIGATING FILE EXPLORER

There are many different sections in the File Explorer. **Windows 11** sees the removal of the ribbon bar, and instead, **you will find a command bar with several useful tools including Cut, Copy, Paste, Rename, Share, Delete, View and Sort icons.**

- **View:** Select different ways to see your folders. You can choose to view large icons or a list with additional details like file sizes and formats.

- **Sort:** Select how you want to arrange all the content in the libraries. choose between alphabetical order, by the last date modified, by the file type, and more. You can also toggle between ascending and descending orders easily.

- **New:** Click to create a new folder, create a shortcut, or create a new document. Several of your most commonly used document formats will show up here including text or Microsoft Word documents, Microsoft Excel spreadsheets, and Microsoft PowerPoint Presentations.

- **See more:** On the right side of the command bar is an icon with three small dots.

This is the "See more" button. Clicking it will reveal a small menu with additional options and features. This includes:

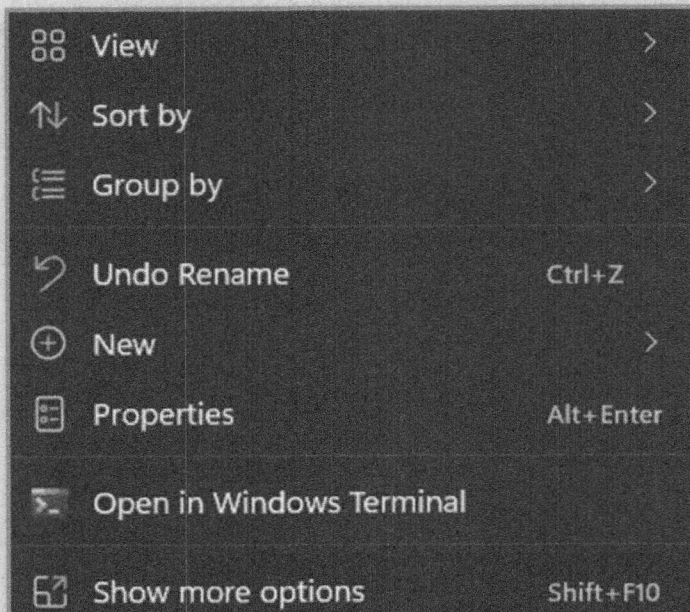

♦ **Undo** - to quickly reverse your most recent actions, which comes in handy if you accidentally delete or move an important document, as well as the ability to select or deselect multiple files.

♦ **Pin files to the Quick Access folder** - places any marked files or folders into a special library which will appear on the left hand side of your screen when working in File Explorer.

♦ **Some of the options in the command bar will change depending on which library you are viewing.** When looking at images, you will see specific image-related tools such as 'rotate' or "set as desktop background." When looking at your drives, you will see tools for networking.

♦ **Other tools** include file cleanup, the option to optimize or format your drives, add a new network location, map a network drive, disconnect a network drive, bring up the file or folder properties or open up the file or folder options.

When right-clicking on any file or folder within the File Explorer, a context menu is brought up. The context menus have also been updated with some new useful tools now being pinned to the top, including the Cut, Copy, Rename, Share, and Delete tools. These are represented by simple icons rather than text.

The new 'Share' feature enables you to easily share content with commonly used contacts much like you would on a mobile device. By clicking the 'share' button you will see a menu pop-up detailing how many items you are sharing, giving you the option to send it to nearby contacts using Bluetooth, to email it using the Mail app, or to use a selection of other apps to share the content.

HOW TO COPY AND PASTE FILES OR FOLDERS

In Windows 11, copying and pasting files is easier than ever before. With the addition of the copy and paste buttons in the Command bar, you simply need to select and highlight the files you wish to have copied and then press the Copy button.

This will save the content onto the 'clipboard.' You can also do this by selecting and highlighting the content and then pressing **Ctrl+C** on your keyboard. Next, navigate to the location where you want to have the files or folders pasted and simply click the Paste button in the command bar.

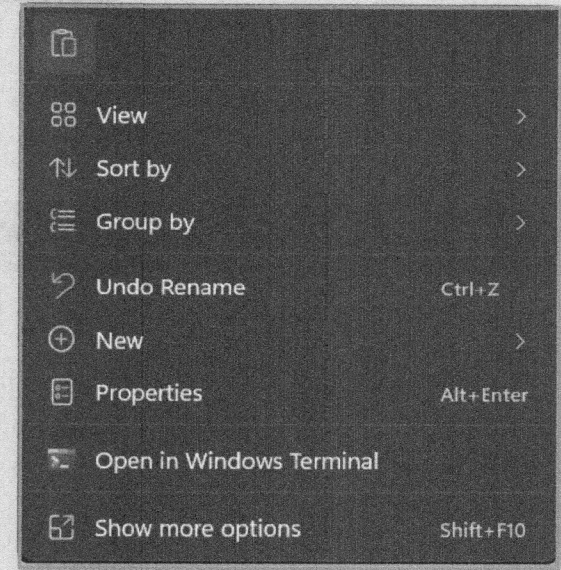

You can also do this by pressing **Ctrl+V** on your keyboard. This will place a copy of the desired content into a new location. Copying and pasting does not alter the original folders or files and you will still be able to see and access them in the original location.

CUTTING FILES AND FOLDERS

The cutting tool is used to remove files or folders from your libraries, but this content is also saved into the clipboard so that it can be pasted into a different location. It works in the same way as the copying tool.

You simply need to select the files or folders that you want removed, click the cut button. You can also use your keyboard to cut files and folders by using **Ctrl+X.** Next, move to the new location and paste the content. It is important to keep in mind that cutting the content will remove it from the original location and it will not produce a duplicate. Cutting is useful to avoid the production of unnecessary duplicates that can clutter up your libraries.

HOW TO SEE THE FILE PROPERTIES

The file properties tell you important information like the name of the file, the type of file such as Word document or Excel spreadsheet or JPEG image, the contents of the folder if it contains many subfolders or multiple files, the size telling you how much space it takes up on your disk drive, the parent folder in which the folder or file is located, the amount of free space in the parent folder of your selected folder, and the time and date of when the file or folder was last accessed and modified.

You can access the file or folder properties by selecting it in the File Explorer, and then pressing the "show more" button in the command line. Remember, this is the button with three dots. **This will bring up a small menu where you can find 'Properties' at the bottom.** You can also show the file or folder properties by selecting and then right clicking directly on it, then scrolling to the bottom of the pop-up menu and selecting 'properties.'

HOW TO USE THE VIEW BUTTON

In Windows 11 you can easily switch between different types of views using the View button in the Command bar. You can choose to view extra large icons, large icons, medium icons, small icons, lists, details, tiles or content. You can also switch to "Compact view" which minimizes the amount of space between files and folders. This feature has been included because Windows 11 is optimized for touch-enabled devices where larger spaces between different files, folders and icons makes it easier to select them when using your finger. However, this feature can easily be enabled or disabled to suit your needs.

In the View menu you can also decide what kind of information you would like to see, including a navigation pane, a details pane, preview pane, item check boxes, file name extensions and hidden items.

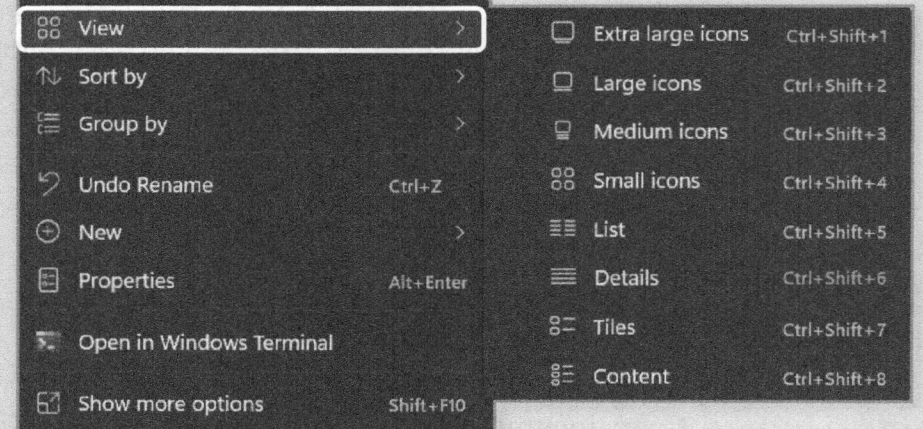

The Navigation pane appears on the left side of the window and provides shortcuts to some of the parent libraries on your computer, including the "Quick Access" library, 'OneDrive,' "This PC," and your 'Network.' Within "Quick Access" you can find the Desktop, Downloads, Documents, Pictures, Music and Videos. You can choose to show or hide the Navigation Pane entirely.

The Details Pane and Preview Pane work similarly to the Navigation pane though they will show up on the right side of the File Explorer Window. These panes will show you information about the file or folder you have selected. The Details Pane shows information such as the name, file format, last date modified, size, and date that your selected folder or file was created. The Preview Pane, as the name suggests, will show you a preview of the selected file. You can scroll through the preview to see different pages in the document using this feature.

The "Item check boxes" feature is a new feature to Windows 11 implemented with touch-screens in mind. It allows you to select multiple files or folders so that you can move, copy, paste or cut them. By clicking this button you will see small check boxes appear over all the items in your File Explorer which can be checked or unchecked. This feature works in exactly the same way as holding down the Ctrl button would while using your mouse to click on multiple items.

Windows 11 also offers you the option to show or hide the file extensions in the File Explorer. The file extensions reveal the file format, which lets Windows know what kind

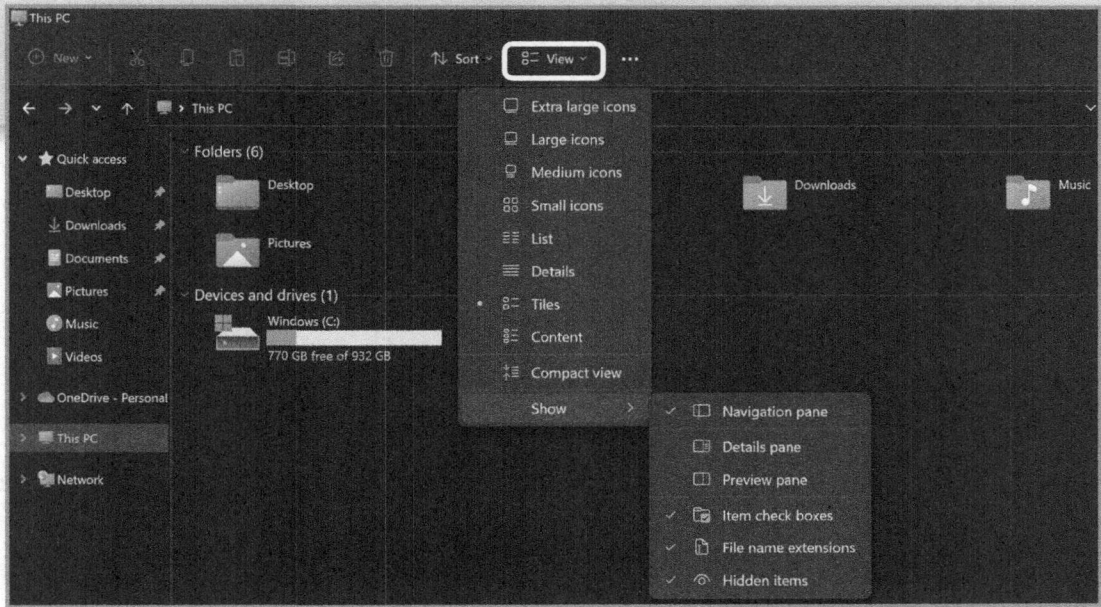

_ □ ✕

of file it is dealing with and which application is needed to open and work or run the file. File extensions are three or four letters long, usually found right at the end of a file's name. They include JPEG, JPG, PNG, DOC, DOCX, XLS, PPT, or ZIP, though there are many others.

Finally you can also choose to view or hide "Hidden items" using the View Menu. Windows offers the ability to hide certain files and folders, and many are hidden by default, because these are not meant to be modified. They often include important system-related data, though any file can be hidden. You can toggle this feature to show or hide these files using the "Hidden items" button.

HOW TO USE THE SORT BUTTON

The Sort button performs in the same way as previous versions of Windows, allowing you to arrange the content in your File Explorer in a few different ways. You can choose to sort your files and folders by name, file type, size, date created, date modified, authors, tags or title. You can also choose whether you want to view the sorted content in ascending or descending order. For example, files can be viewed by size from largest to smallest, or from smallest to largest. Similarly **you can view content from A-Z or Z-A.**

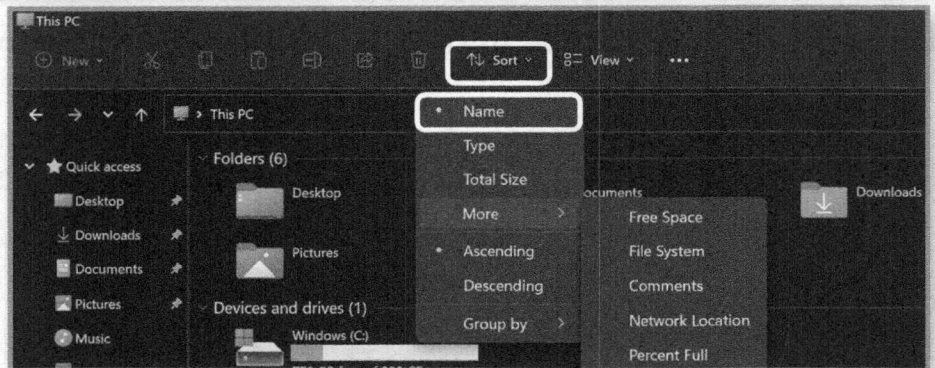

_ □ ✕

HOW TO CREATE A NEW FOLDER

Creating a new folder in File Explorer is easier than ever. You simply need to click the 'New' button in the left side of the Command Bar. This will present you with a drop-down menu giving you the option to create either a new folder or shortcut. This

21°C
Sunny intervals

12:00 AM
01/01/2022

menu will also allow you to create a range of new files including Microsoft Word documents, Microsoft Excel spreadsheets or Microsoft PowerPoint presentations. This action will open up the relevant program so that you can begin working on the new document.

HOW TO MOVE A FILE FROM ONE FOLDER TO ANOTHER

There are a few ways that you can use the Windows 11 File Explorer to move files from one location to another. **The first step is to select the file or files that you wish to move. You can do this by holding down the Ctrl button while clicking on your desired files, or you can select the files using the checkboxes mentioned earlier.** Make sure that your desired files are correctly highlighted before moving them which can be done in two main ways:

The first is to simply drag and drop the files into your desired location. This method works best if you are using a typical computer or laptop with a mouse. Click on the selected files which should be highlighted and drag them over to the folder where you want them to be placed.

You can also copy and paste your files from one location to another. This can be done using the keyboard shortcuts Ctrl+C and Ctrl+V or the copy and paste buttons that are found on the control bar. You can also choose to cut and paste instead, which will delete the files from their original location rather than producing duplicates.

HOW TO DELETE A FILE OR FOLDER

You can delete a folder or file in File Explorer by selecting it, and then pressing the 'Delete' button in the Command Bar. You can also right-click on any files or folders you want to delete which will bring up a small menu where you will also find an option to 'delete.'

‒ ☐ ✕

You can also press Maiusc + Canc button both, to delete definitively a single or multiple files. Pay attention, in this case, you won't recover that file/files on the recycle bin.

HOW TO FIND A FILE ON YOUR COMPUTER

File Explorer makes it easy to find a file or folder no matter where it is stored on your computer. **Below the Command bar you will see an Address bar on the left and a Search bar on the right.** All you need to do is type the name of the file or folder that you are looking for into this search bar. Your search results will be displayed in the File Explorer window.

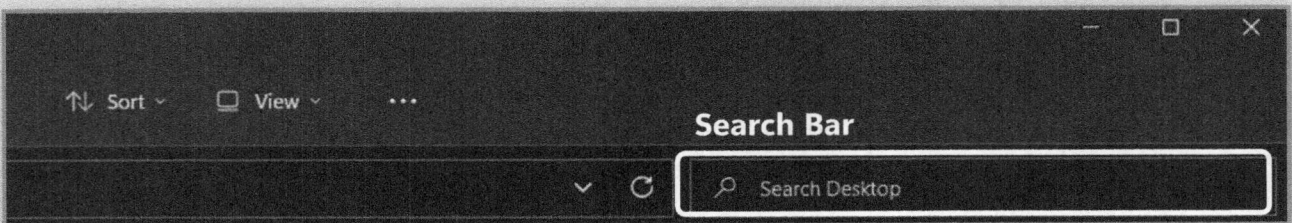

HOW TO UNDO OR REDO AN ACTION

If you accidentally delete a file or move something to a location by mistake, you can easily undo this action using your keyboard shortcuts. **Simply press Ctrl+Z to undo an action, and Ctrl+Y to redo it.**

HOW TO RECOVER A DELETED FILE OR FOLDER

Windows 11, like in previous versions, will keep a temporary copy of all deleted files and folders in the Recycle Bin.

Recycle Bin

To open the Recycle Bin you can click on the icon found on your desktop, or you can find it by typing "Recycle Bin" in the address bar of the File Explorer. Recycle Bin will open a folder in your File Explorer, showing all of the files and folders which have been recently deleted.

Navigate to the file or folder you wish to restore, click on it, and you will see a button in

the Command bar giving you the option to restore this file. This action will place the file back into the original location where you can access it.

If you cannot find an icon for the Recycle Bin on your desktop, you may need to change a few settings.

1. **OPEN ⚙ SETTINGS > PERSONALIZATION > THEMES.**
2. **Scroll to "Desktop icon settings."**
3. **Here, make sure that the Recycle Bin checkbox is checked.**

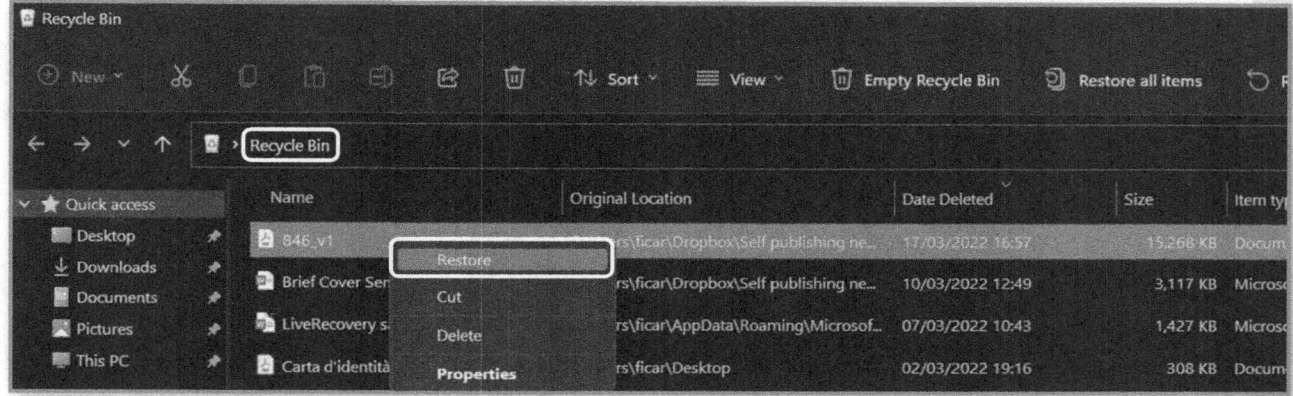

CHAPTER 2:

HOW TO MANAGE THE SETTINGS

_ □ ✕

Windows 11 allows you to change and alter many of the settings to have a more customized and personal experience when working or playing on your computer. This chapter will look at how to use and change some of the most important settings.

🔍 **THE SETTINGS APP**

The Settings App takes over from the Control Panel in Windows 11 and is the central hub for all your customization, installation, connectivity, account settings, and more. You can find the Settings App in many ways:

- **Click on the Start Menu ▦ and navigate to the Settings icon ⚙** indicated by a cogwheel.

   ♦ You can drag and drop this icon onto your taskbar to pin the Settings App for easy access. You can also pin the Settings App to the taskbar by right-clicking the app icon and selecting **"Pin to taskbar."**

- **Click on the Start Menu ▦ and type in 'settings'** to bring up the Settings app icon.

- **Click on the Start Menu ▦ and click on the "All apps" button**. You can then search for the Settings App, sorted amongst the other apps in alphabetical order.

- The Settings App can also be opened using the **keyboard shortcut: Windows Key ▦ + I**.

21°C
Sunny intervals

12:00 AM
01/01/2022

_ ☐ ✕

- Finally, you can click on the Quick Settings button on the right side of the taskbar, which will bring up a small flyout menu, where an icon for the full Settings App can be found in the lower right corner.

The Settings App features different categories of settings in a navigation pane on the left side of the window and automatically opens up onto the Systems settings.

This section will include the following options: Display, Sound, Notifications, Focus Assistant, Power And Battery, Storage, Nearby Sharing, Multitasking, Activation, Troubleshoot, Recovery, Projecting To This PC, Remote Desktop, Clipboard and About.

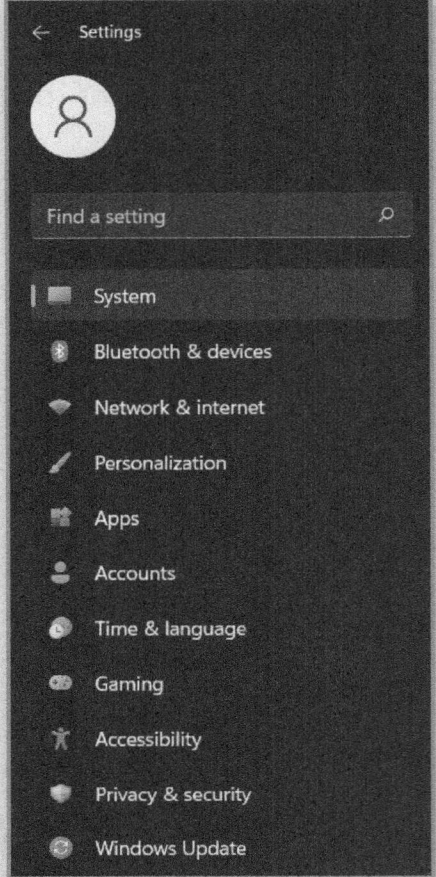

SYSTEM

- Display
- Sound
- Notifications
- Focus assist
- Power & battery
- Storage
- Activation
- Troubleshoot
- Recovery
- Projecting to this PC
- Remote Desktop
- Clipboard
- About

BLUETOOTH & DEVICES

- Bluetooth
- Devices
- Printers & scanners
- Your phone
- Cameras
- Mouse
- Touchpad
- Touch
- Pen & Windows Ink
- AutoPlay
- USB

NETWORK & INTERNET

- Wi-Fi
- VPN
- Mobile hotspot
- Airplane mode
- Proxy
- Dial-up
- Advanced network settings

PERSONALIZATION

- Background
- Colors
- Themes
- Lock screen
- Touch keyboard
- Start
- Taskbar
- Fonts
- Device usage

APPS

- Apps & features
- Default apps
- Offline maps
- Optional features
- Apps for websites
- Video playback
- Startup

ACCOUNTS

- Your Microsoft account
- Your info
- Email & accounts
- Sign-in options
- Family & other users
- Windows backup
- Access work or school

TIME & LANGUAGE

- Date & time
- Language & region
- Typing
- Speech

21°C
Sunny intervals

12:00 AM
01/01/2022

GAMING

- Xbox Game Bar
- Captures
- Game Mode

PRIVACY & SECURITY

- **Security**
  - ◊ Windows Security
  - ◊ Find my device
  - ◊ Device encryption
  - ◊ For developers

- **Windows permissions**
  - ◊ General
  - ◊ Speech
  - ◊ Inking & typing personalization
  - ◊ Diagnostics & feedback
  - ◊ Activity history
  - ◊ Search permissions

WINDOWS UPDATE

- Pause updates
- Update history
- Advanced options
- Windows Insider Program

ACCESSIBILITY

- **Vision**
  - ◊ Text size
  - ◊ Visual effects
  - ◊ Mouse pointer and touch
  - ◊ Text cursor
  - ◊ Magnifier
  - ◊ Color filters
  - ◊ Contrast themes
  - ◊ Narrator

- **Hearing**
  - ◊ Audio
  - ◊ Captions

- **Interaction**
  - ◊ Speech
  - ◊ Keyboard
  - ◊ Mouse
  - ◊ Eye control

ACCOUNTS

Since the release of Windows 10, Microsoft has been encouraging its users to use their Microsoft accounts to log in to their computers and laptops.

_ □ X

A Microsoft account is a free account associated with a Microsoft email address and linked to online services such as OneDrive, Xbox Live, Skype, and Microsoft 365. You need an internet connection to use all the features associated with a Microsoft account. In comparison, you can also use a "local account" to log in to your computer; this is the traditional way of logging into your computer and is not linked to any email address or online services. It involves only a username and password which will be stored on your PC.

There are several benefits to using a Microsoft account, including access to some of the online services mentioned previously. It automatically enables full-disk encryption of your system drive, allowing you to safely store and secure all your computer's data on OneDrive.

Your subscription and activation data will be stored with your Microsoft account so that if you need to reinstall Windows, you will not need to buy a new copy, and you can also sync your settings across multiple devices. Using your Microsoft account means that your Mail, Calendar, and other downloaded apps will automatically sync with the associated email address. Finally, you can quickly recover your password through your emails with a Microsoft account, whereas recovering a password for a local account is much more difficult.

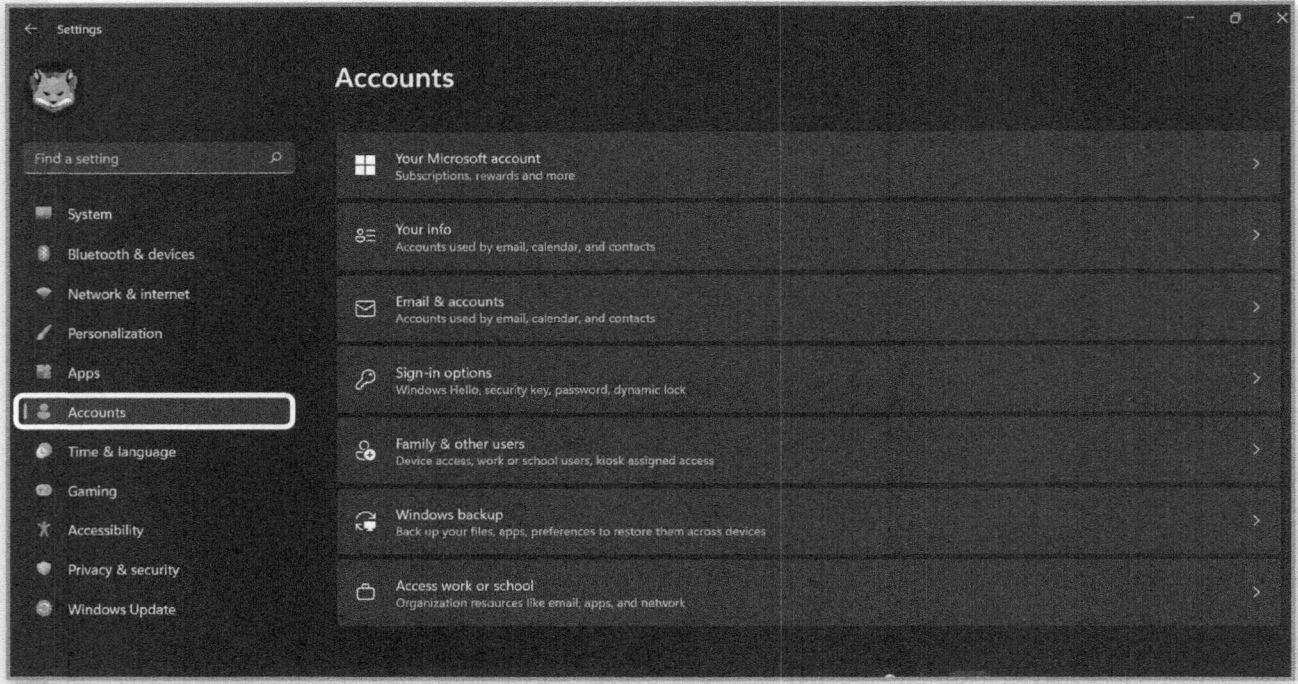

21°C
Sunny intervals

12:00 AM
01/01/2022

_ ☐ ✕

HOW TO CREATE A MICROSOFT ACCOUNT

You will need a Microsoft account and an internet connection to begin using Windows 11 after it has been installed on your device. **If you do not have a Microsoft account, you can easily create one. You can do this by visiting the Microsoft website at signup.live. com or following the steps during your Windows 11 installation process.**

You can use an existing email address or get a new one from Microsoft by selecting "Get a new email address." This will direct you to a form to fill in your name, date of birth, gender, and set a username. You will be asked to choose a strong password. That's it!

Upon your fresh installation of Windows 11, all you need to do is use this account when signing in.

HOW TO CREATE A NEW LOCAL ACCOUNT

Windows 11 does not allow you to carry out the installation without a Microsoft account for security reasons. However, once the operating system is installed, you can change your settings so that you can sign into the device using a local account instead.

TO DO THIS, YOU NEED TO VISIT ⚙ SETTINGS APP > ACCOUNT > YOUR INFO.

You will find a link that says, **"Sign in with a local account instead"**. Click on this link, and it will direct you to a window asking you to sign out of your Microsoft account and verify your identity before setting up a local account. You can select a username for your local account, and though a password is not required, it is strongly suggested.

The next step is to click sign-out, which will log you out of your Microsoft account, and then you can sign back into your device using the new local account settings that you just created.

SIGN-IN OPTIONS

Once you have successfully linked a Microsoft account to your device, Windows 11 offers a few different ways **to sign in securely using Windows Hello**.

This includes a password, a PIN code, facial recognition, or fingerprint scanner.

You can choose how you want to sign in by visiting:

_ ☐ ✕

■ START > ⚙ SETTINGS APP > ACCOUNTS > SIGN-IN OPTIONS > SET UP > GET STARTED.

You will be asked to **create a 4-digit PIN code** or enter an existing PIN code to confirm your identity.

Then simply follow the prompts on the screen to set up your computer's facial recognition or fingerprint scanning services if your device has the relevant hardware.

CHANGING YOUR WINDOWS HELLO PIN

You can change the 4-digit PIN used by Windows Hello for signing into your device by visiting:

START > ⚙ SETTINGS > ACCOUNTS > SIGN-IN OPTIONS.

In this window, **click on PIN > Change PIN.** You will have to input your old PIN to verify your identity before selecting a new one.

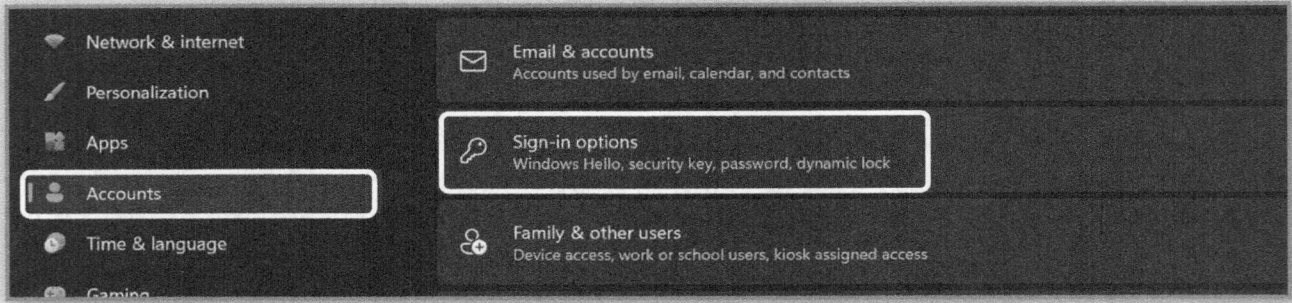

CHANGE YOUR MICROSOFT ACCOUNT PASSWORD

Microsoft has been urging its consumers to move away from using passwords to sign into their devices, encouraging the use of alternatives like the PIN system. This is because of the security measures put in place and the fact that many users use the same password for their email and device logins.

This means that if you have enabled any of the Windows Hello sign-in options, you will not be able to change your Microsoft account password in the following way.
To change your Microsoft account password, visit:

21°C
Sunny intervals

12:00 AM
01/01/2022

_ ☐ ✕

⚙ **SETTINGS > ACCOUNTS > SIGN-IN OPTIONS > PASSWORD, THEN SELECT "CHANGE YOUR PASSWORD."**

Next, you will need to input your existing password before entering a new password and a password hint to help you remember it.

If you have enabled Windows Hello sign-in options, you can only change your Microsoft account password by visiting the Microsoft website at **account.microsoft.com.**

There you click "Change password: security." Verify your identity by selecting your Microsoft account and inputting the one-time code that will be sent to the linked address. Then you can enter your old password before typing a new password. You will also need to select a password hint to help you remember it in the future. Then click Finish to apply your changes.

_ ☐ ✕

🔍 PERSONALIZATION SETTINGS

You can easily access any personalization settings by right-clicking on your Desktop and selecting Personalization from the pop-up menu. Alternatively, you can find Personalization settings in your Settings app.

HOW TO CUSTOMIZE THE TASKBAR

The Taskbar is locked to the bottom of the screen in Windows 11; however, you can make many other changes to suit your liking.

_ □ ✕

ALIGN TASKBAR ITEMS TO THE LEFT

If you prefer the more traditional left-aligned layout of the Windows Taskbar, you can apply the following settings:

⚙ **SETTINGS APP > PERSONALIZATION > TASKBAR > TASKBAR BEHAVIORS.**

Here you can find the option to align the icons on the left or in the center of the screen. Auto-Hide the Taskbar

You can choose to apply the auto-hide setting to your taskbar so that it disappears from the screen while you are not using it. It will reappear when you move your mouse to the bottom of the screen. This setting is also found in the **"Taskbar behaviors" settings.**

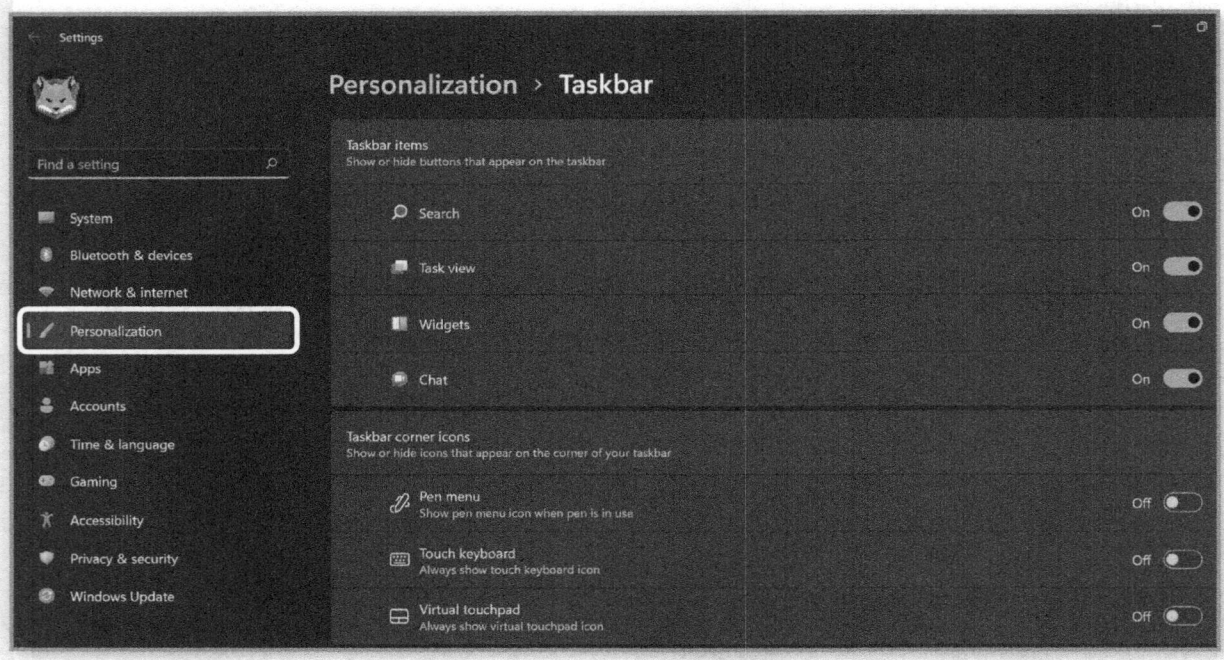

_ □ ✕

CHANGE THE COLOR OF THE TASKBAR

You can change the color of your taskbar or make it transparent.

 21°C
Sunny intervals

 12:00 AM
01/01/2022

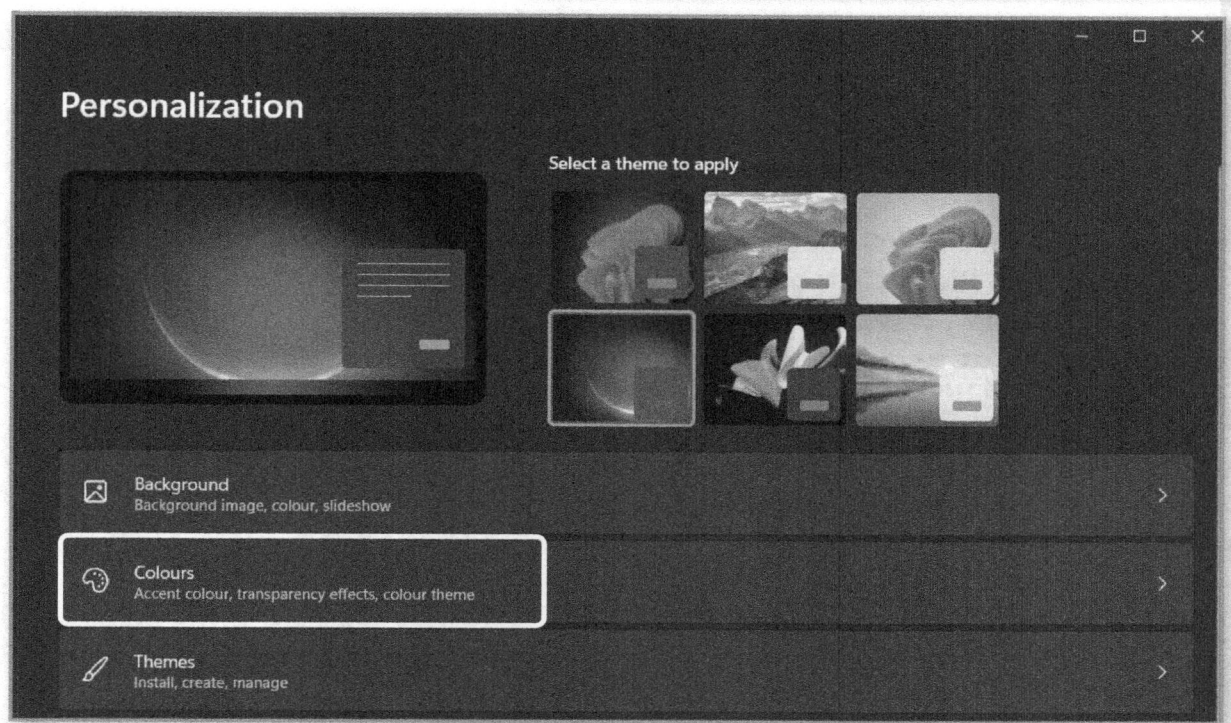

You can find these settings in:

⚙ SETTINGS > PERSONALIZATION > COLORS.

You will need to **select the 'Custom' option** from the "Choose your mode" drop-down menu and **'Dark'** from the **"Choose your default Windows mode"** menu.

Next, scroll down and toggle the **"Show accent color on Start and Taskbar"** option. Then set the color accent option to **'Manual'** and pick your color from the available options.

PIN APPS TO THE TASKBAR

You can pin apps to the taskbar for quick and easy access. To do this, **find the app in "All apps" within the Start menu.**

Right-click on the icon and then select "Pin to taskbar". If you do not see this option, you should see **'More'.** Click on this button and select **"Pin to Taskbar".**

_ ☐ ✕

You can also pin apps **from your Desktop to the taskbar by right-clicking on the icon and selecting the option "Pin to Taskbar".**

Similarly, if you have an app open and running, you will see its icon in the taskbar, with a line underneath it. **Right-click on this icon and select "Pin to Taskbar".**

REMOVE AN APP FROM THE TASKBAR

Removing an app from the taskbar is as easy as right-clicking on the icon and selecting the option to "Unpin from taskbar".

Some icons cannot be removed from the taskbar; this includes the Start Menu, Search, Task View, Widgets, and Chat. The latter four apps can be hidden from view. To hide these apps visit:

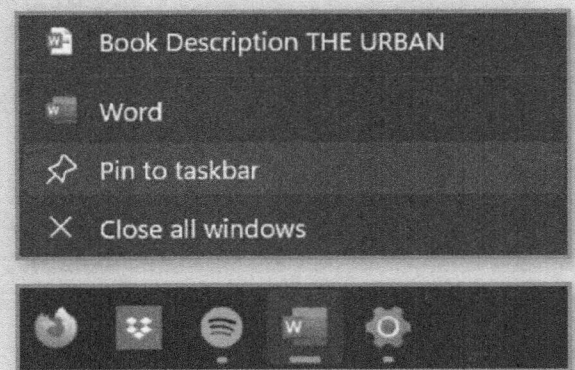

⚙ **SETTINGS APP > PERSONALIZATION > TASKBAR**, where you will see taskbar items. You can toggle the sliders on the right-hand side to hide these app icons from the taskbar.

SHOW BADGES IN THE TASKBAR

Certain apps will display badges that you can choose to hide; this includes the Chat app, which will display a counter for all your unread messages. You can toggle this setting off in the "Taskbar behavior" settings.

CHANGE TASKBAR CORNER

The taskbar corner is found on the right side of the taskbar and has small icons for important functions like keyboard, battery, volume, and language settings. The taskbar corner is designed to reduce clutter while still giving you quick access to various settings.

Clicking on the taskbar overflow corner will bring up the Quick Settings flyout menu where you can see the full list of icons and their status. The default settings include internet connectivity, Bluetooth, flight mode, battery save, focus assistant, accessibility,

21°C
Sunny intervals

12:00 AM
01/01/2022

_ ☐ ✕

cast, volume and brightness settings.

At the bottom of the flyout menu you will see a pencil icon and a cogwheel icon. The pencil icon allows you to pin or unpin settings from this menu, while the cogwheel will open up the full Settings app.

Some icons can be enabled or disabled from the system tray such as the Pen menu, Touch menu, and Visual touchpad. This is useful if you do not use these input options on your device. To enable or disable these icons, visit:

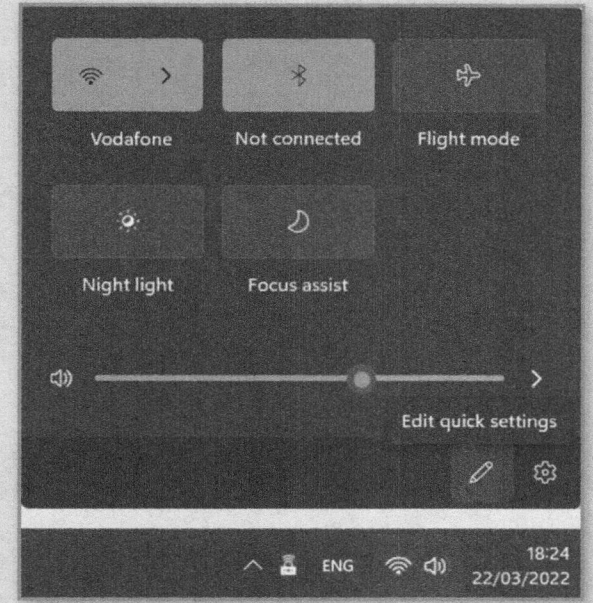

⚙ **SETTINGS > PERSONALIZATION > TASKBAR;** then you can toggle these settings on or off.

Within the Taskbar corner is the overflow tray, which is accessed by clicking the small up arrow. You can change which icon apps you want to have displayed in this overflow tray in the taskbar settings under Taskbar corner overflow.

🔍 HOW TO CUSTOMIZE THE START MENU

Add or Remove Pinned Apps
To add an app to your Start menu, locate the app icon by opening "All apps" in the Start menu. When you find the app you are looking for, right-click on the icon and select "Pin to Start." Similarly, to remove an app that is pinned to the Start menu, right-click on its icon and select "Unpin from Start." (See the image in the next page)

Choose which folders appear on Start Next to the power button
You can set some icon that will be show next to power button in start menu. It's very simple, visit:

⚙ **SETTINGS MENU >PERSONALIZATION>START>FOLDERS** and click on the folders that you usually use. (See the image in the next page)

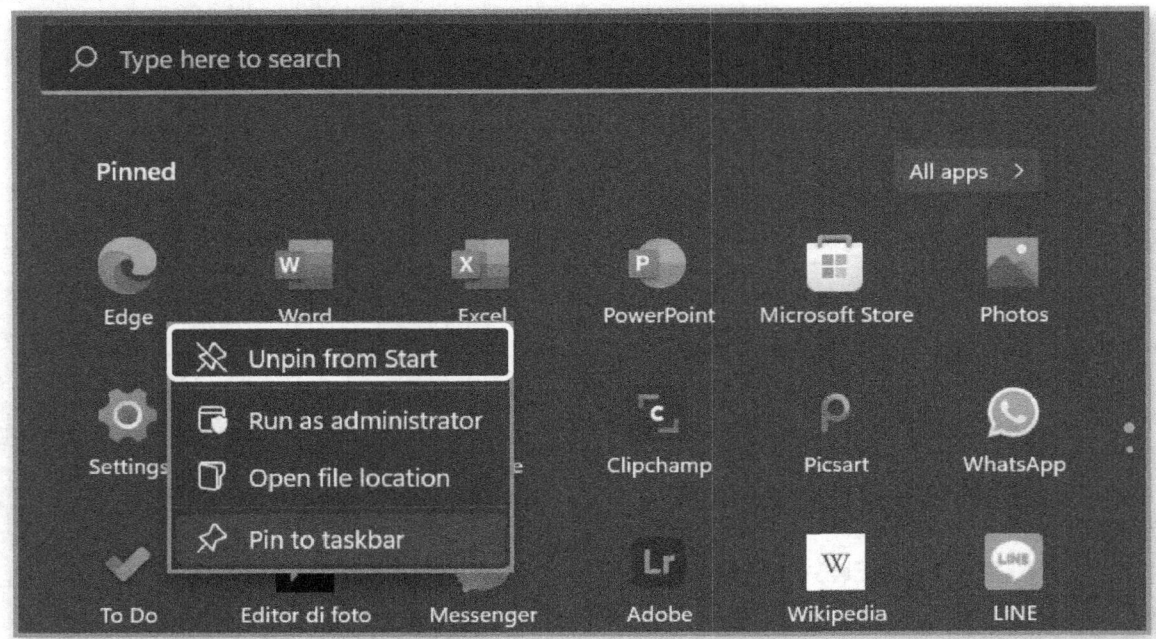

Add or Remove Pinned Apps

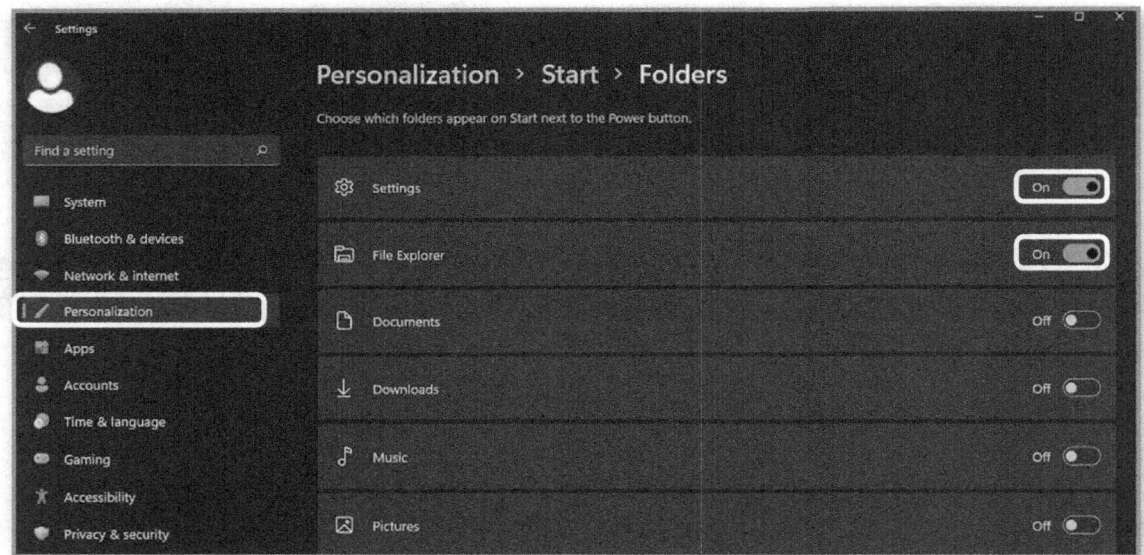

Choose which folders appear on Start Next to the power button. After that, you will see icons here:

— ☐ ✕

CHANGE THE START MENU COLOR

When you apply changes to the color of your taskbar, they will also apply to the Start menu. To make these changes, **visit the Settings app's Personalization tab and select 'Colors.'**

You will need to select the 'Custom' option from the **"Choose your mode" drop-down menu and 'Dark' from the "Choose your default Windows mode" menu.** Next, scroll down and toggle the option for **"Show accent color on Start and Taskbar".**

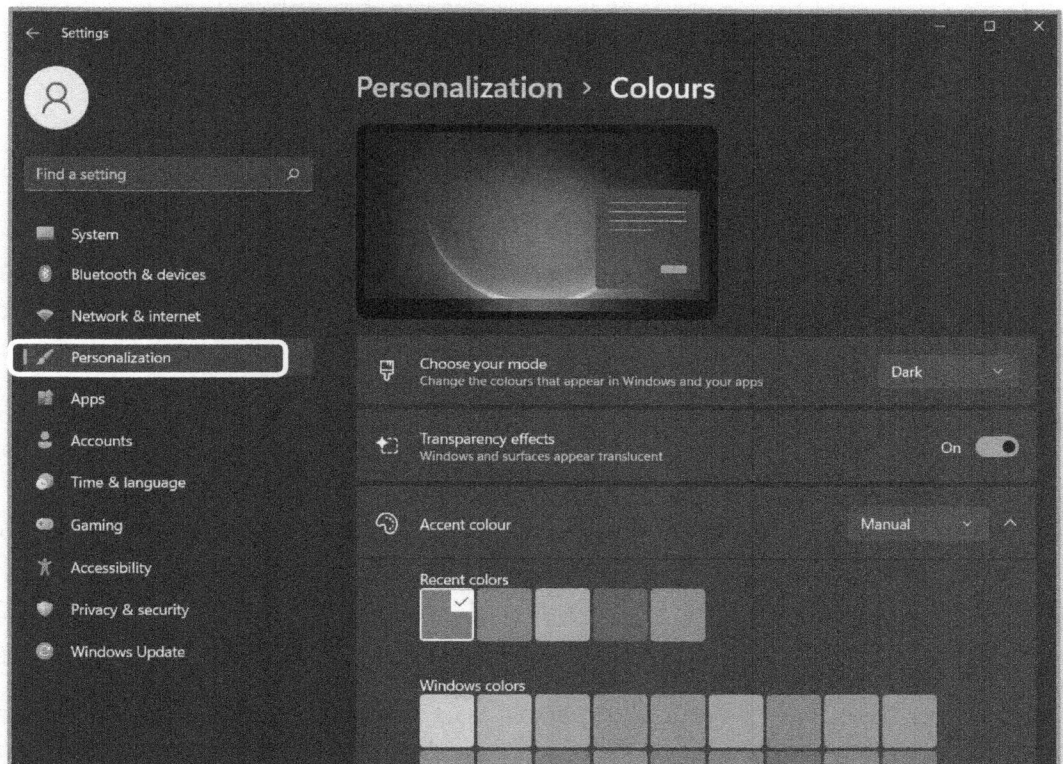

— ☐ ✕

Please note: Disable the transparency effects if you PC running slow during opening and closing apps or folders. This function it overloads the gpu and may slow down your pc. Try disabling it to make your PC faster and smoother.

_ □ ✕

HIDE THE RECOMMENDED ITEMS, MOST USED, AND RECENTLY INSTALLED APPS

Windows 11 will show recently added and most used apps in the Start menu by default. You can hide these apps in the ⚙ **SETTINGS APP by clicking PERSONALIZATION > START**. Here, you can toggle these settings to your liking.

PIN LIBRARIES

Unfortunately, you cannot pin files or folders to the Start menu in Windows 11. However, you can pin your libraries, including File Explorer, Documents, Downloads, Music, Pictures, and Videos. All you need to do is visit the ⚙ **SETTINGS APP**, select:

PERSONALIZATION > START > FOLDERS, and toggle the libraries you wish to have pinned to the Start menu to the 'On' position.

HOW TO CUSTOMIZE THE LOCK SCREEN

When your Windows 11 device is locked, you will see the Lock Screen showing the time and date over a background wallpaper. To change the appearance of your Lock Screen, you need to use the ⚙ **SETTINGS APP** and choose:

PERSONALIZATION > LOCK SCREEN. Here you can find three main options:

1. **Personalize your lock screen:** this option allows you to select an image for your background wallpaper on the lock screen. You can choose an image from your Picture Library or use a slideshow of multiple images. You can also select Windows Spotlight, which will automatically import an image from Bing that will be updated and changed regularly.

2. **Lock screen status:** this option lets you decide what information to show on your Lock Screen using one of the Windows 11 apps. You can choose between 3D Viewer (which works on mobile devices with an accelerometer and creates a 3D Parallax effect), Weather, Amazon, Xbox console companion, Mail, or Calendar. You can only select one of these apps to display information on your lock screen.

3. **Show the lock screen background picture on the sign-in screen:** this option allows you to remove the lock screen background image from being displayed when you enter the sign-in screen.

21°C
Sunny intervals

12:00 AM
01/01/2022

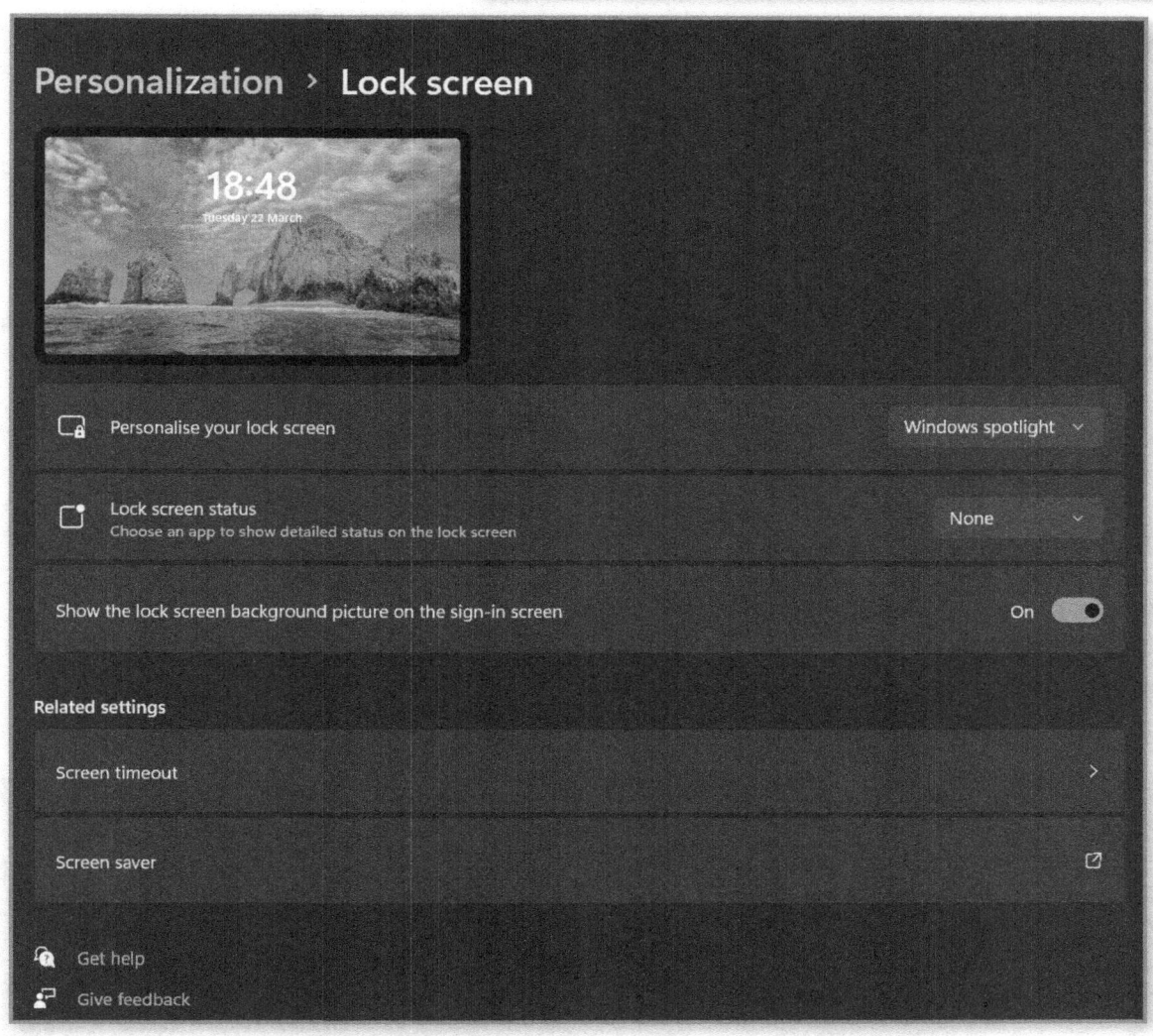

_ ☐ ✕

HOW TO CUSTOMIZE THE DESKTOP BACKGROUND

Windows 11 makes it easy to change your Desktop background. All you need to do is open ⚙ **SETTINGS > PERSONALIZATION,** and then **SELECT BACKGROUND**.

In this menu, you will find **"Personalize your background",** where you can choose Pictures or Slideshow from the drop-down menu. You can select one of the built-in wallpaper images or browse for your image.

You can also decide how you want the picture to fit on your Desktop, depending on the image's dimensions and your monitor.

If you would like to have a slideshow of images set as your Desktop background, you can easily create an album for this purpose in the settings app. There are also options for how often the picture should change and whether the order of images should be shuffled.

The Desktop background can also be set to a solid color by choosing "Solid color" instead of 'Slideshow' or 'Picture.'

You can configure different backgrounds for each desktops, for example, if you prefer a plain background for your work desktop but a photograph of your family members for your entertainment desktop. You can access these settings by selecting "Personalize your background" and then Picture.

Right-click on the image you want to set, and it will provide a drop-down menu with options to "Set for all desktops" or "Set for desktop." Choose "Set for desktop," and then select which desktop you want it applied to.

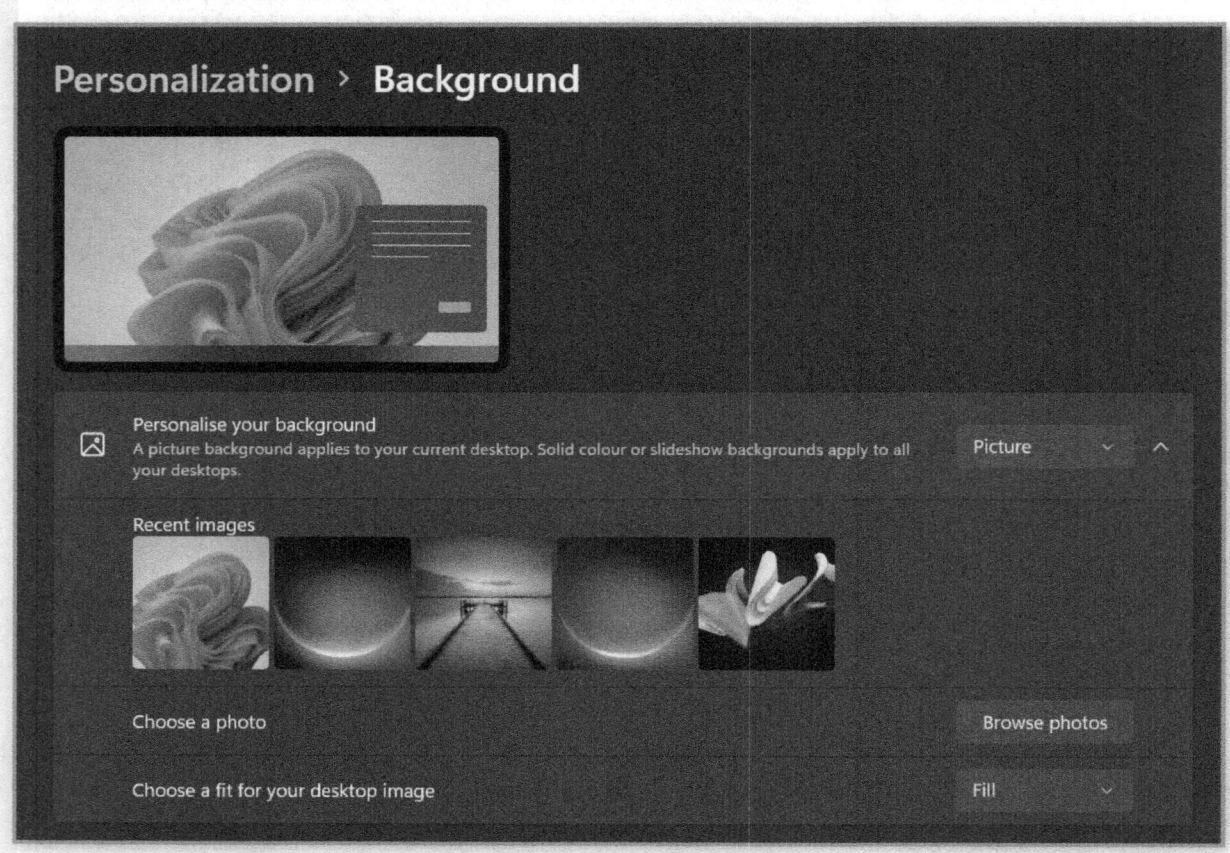

_ □ ✕

🔍 HOW TO CHANGE THE LOOK OF WINDOWS 11

DARK MODE AND LIGHT MODE

Dark mode and light mode change the color of the taskbar, Start menu, desktop background, windows and also the sound schemes.

Dark mode has light text on darker windows and background, with more subdued and softer sounds for different alerts and notifications.

Light mode has dark text on light windows and backgrounds, with more vibrant desktop backgrounds and striking alert and notification sounds.

You can switch between dark mode and light mode by visiting the Personalization section in the ⚙ **Settings app and selecting Colors.** You will see the option to switch between Dark and Light here.

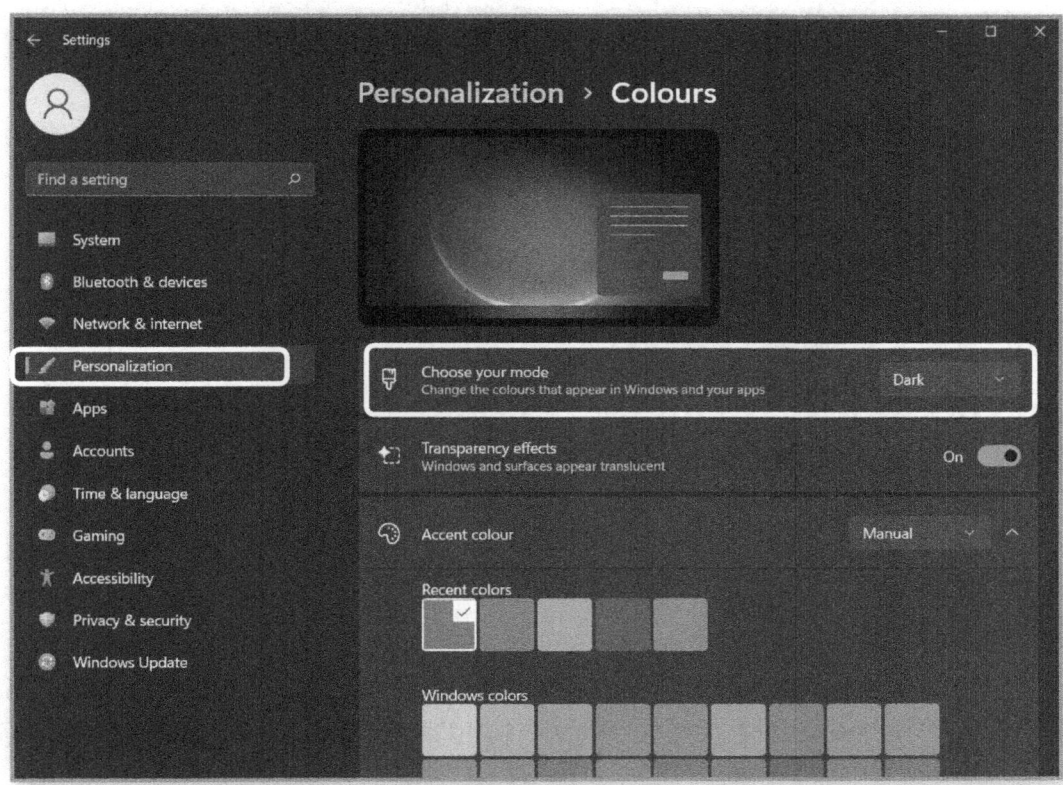

_ ☐ ✕

THEMES

A theme is a group of settings relating to your computer's background wallpaper, colors, sounds, and other personalization options. Windows 11 comes with 6 themes: Windows Dark, Windows Light, Clow, Captured Motion, Sun Rise, and Flow. You can also download additional themes from the Microsoft website.

Themes can be customized by visiting the **Themes section of Personalization settings.** Here you can choose desktop backgrounds, color schemes, sound packages and mouse cursor styles.

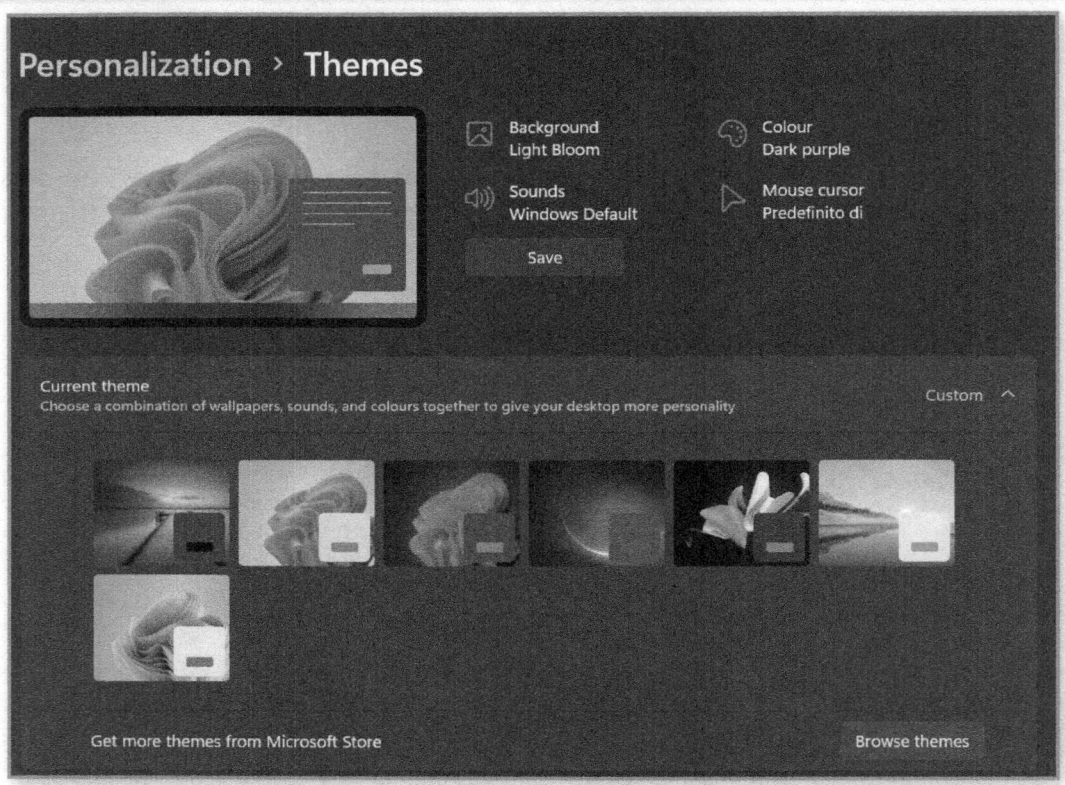

_ ☐ ✕

CUSTOM SCALING

Windows 11 will automatically try to scale the elements on your display so that you can see them easily and clearly. However, there are times when you may wish to increase

21°C
Sunny intervals

12:00 AM
01/01/2022

_ ☐ ✕

the size of the text, icons, and other buttons. For example, some laptops have very high resolutions and this can result in the icons and text being very small even though they may be crystal clear. Similarly, if you use multiple monitors you may find the scaling option on the primary device doesn't work well on the secondary device. **You can easily adjust these scaling options in:**

⚙ **SETTINGS > DISPLAY > SCALE AND LAYOUT.**

Here you can find the Scale and Display resolution options. You can select different scaling options from the drop down menu, though you will see that 100% is always recommended. You can also change the display resolution to fit the dimensions of your monitor. This feature is useful for widescreen monitors.

If you have a mobile device like a tablet, you can also find settings for the Display orientation. This setting is used to switch between landscape and portrait orientations depending on how you want to use your tablet.

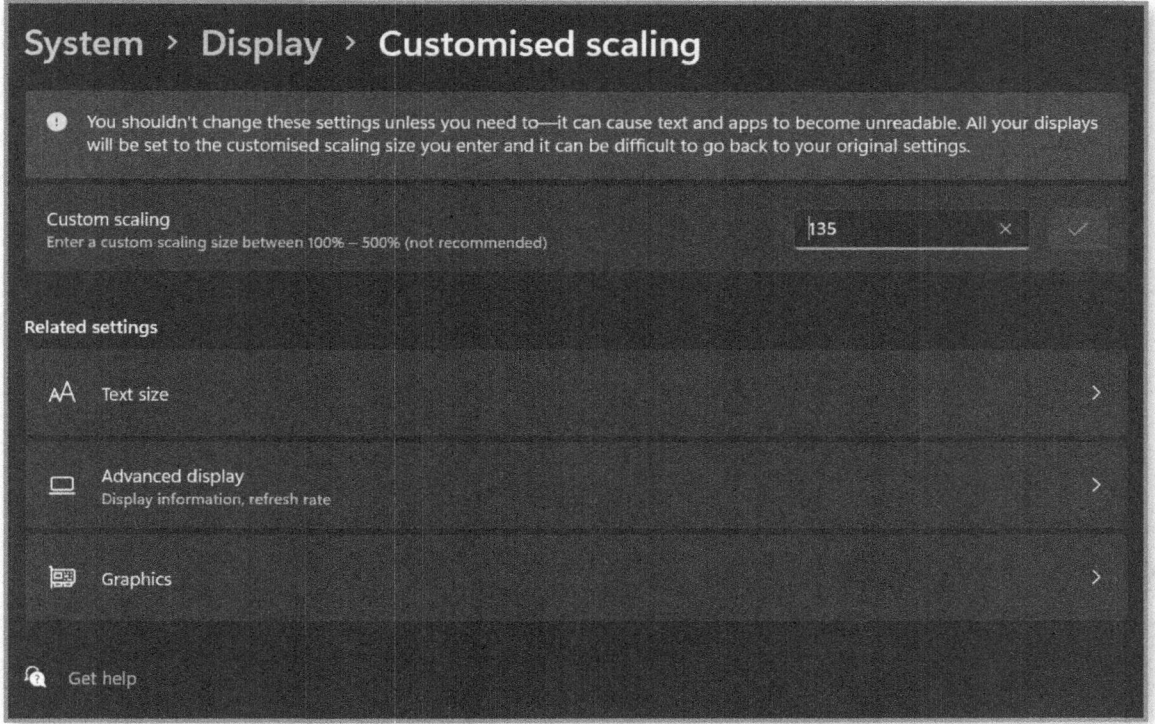

CONTRAST THEMES

Contrast themes have been included in Windows 11 as a way to increase accessibility for people with vision problems though they can be used by anyone. These are designed with a high contrast between different design elements to make text, windows and cursors easier to see.

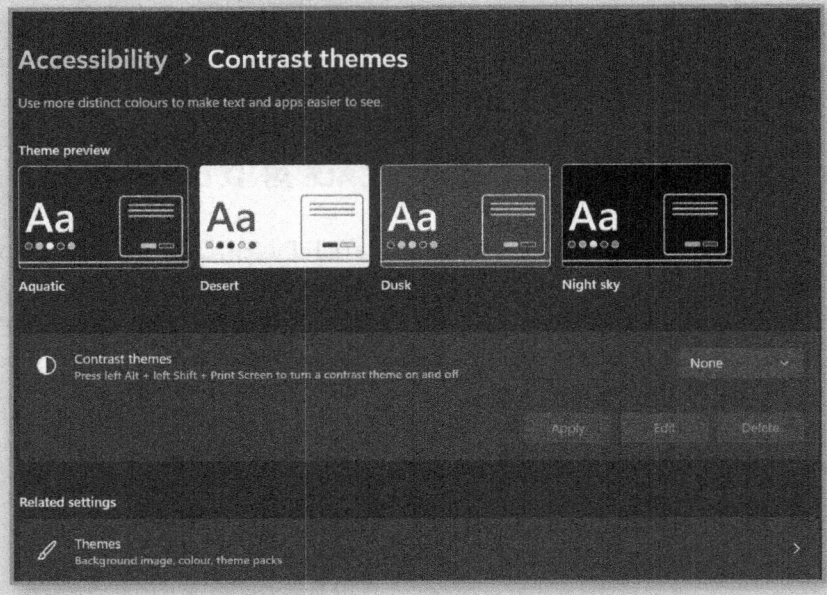

There are 4 default contrast themes: Aquatic, Desert, Dusk, and Night sky. You can access the contrast themes in:

SETTINGS > ACCESSIBILITY > CONTRAST THEMES.

You can also toggle between a high contrast theme and a normal theme by using the keyboard shortcut: Left Alt key + Left Shift key + Print Screen.

OTHER CUSTOMIZATION OPTIONS

TOUCH KEYBOARD

Windows 11 offers a modernized and improved touch keyboard designed for use with touch-enabled devices like tablets and some laptops. It is highly customizable with useful features such as new finger gestures, rounded key corners, a grip tab, better layout, an emoji panel with GIFs and is integrated with the clipboard so you can see items which have been copied.

21°C
Sunny intervals

12:00 AM
01/01/2022

You can find the settings for the touch keyboard in:

PERSONALIZATION > TOUCH KEYBOARD.

Here, you can alter the size of the keyboard or reset it to the default size. You can choose between a few different styling options using the keyboard themes, and you can also include an image for the keyboard background.

Windows 11 offers sixteen different themes including Light, Dark, Color Pop, Tangerine Tides, Lilac River, Indigo Breeze, and Green-Purple.

You can customize each of these themes or create your own by selecting:

KEYBOARD THEMES SETTINGS > CUSTOM THEME OPTION > EDIT.

This feature will allow you to change the text color of the keys, the key background color, the transparency level of the keys, and the background color of the keyboard. You can also select an image to set as the keyboard background.

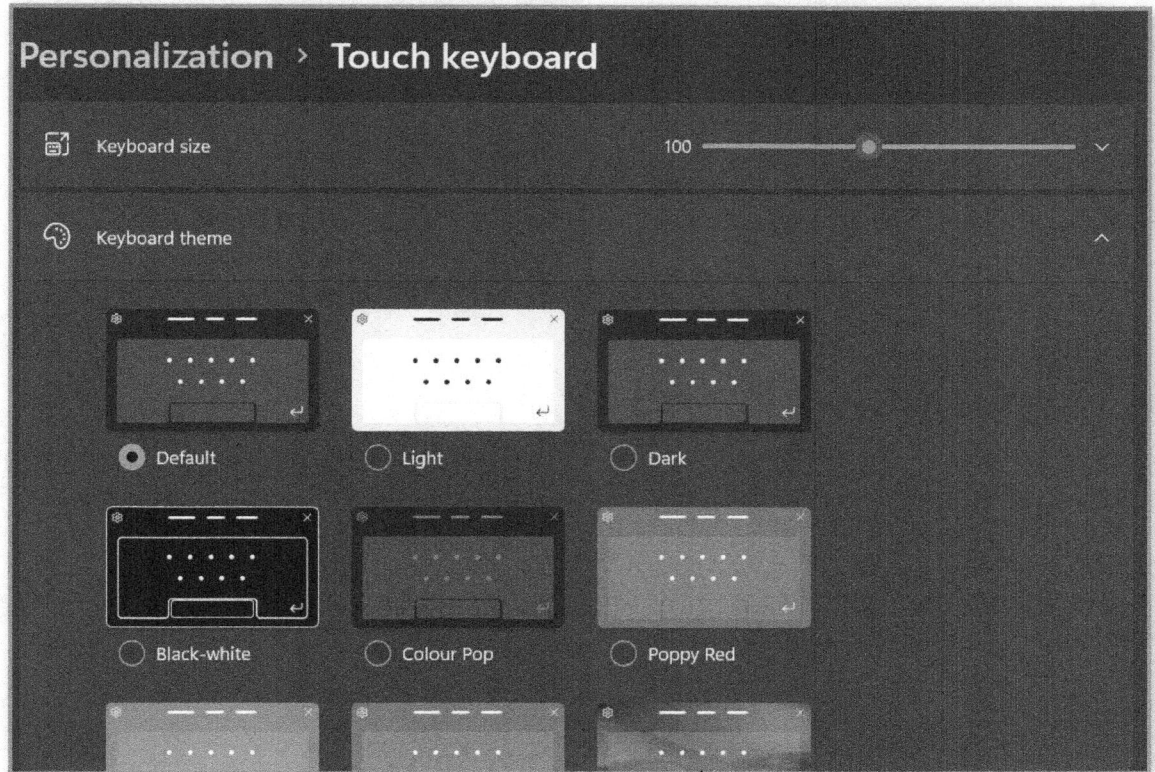

_ □ ✕

FONTS

The default font on Windows 11 is called Segoe and it cannot be changed, however you can adjust the size of the font easily.

To increase the font size go to ⚙ **SETTINGS > ACCESSIBILITY > TEXT SIZE.** This will change the size of the font in all of the windows and applications that you open.

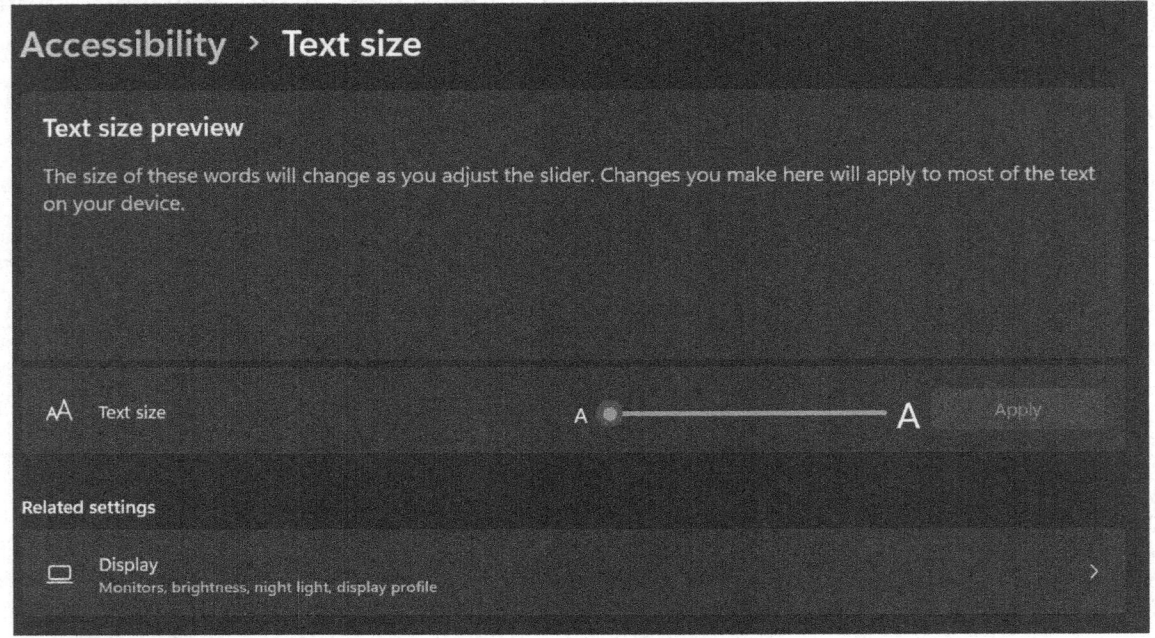

_ □ ✕

VISUAL EFFECTS

Windows 11 comes with certain animations such as shrinking apps into the background when you minimize them. These effects can be distracting or harmful but you can turn these off in the settings.

In the **ACCESSIBILITY SETTINGS** under **VISUAL EFFECTS,** you will be able to toggle settings for Always show the scrollbar, Transparency effects, Animation effects, and Dismiss notifications after this amount of time.

_ □ ✕

MOUSE POINTER AND TOUCH

The appearance of the mouse pointer on your screen can be changed to make it easier to see.

In ⚙ **SETTINGS > ACCESSIBILITY > MOUSE POINTER AND TOUCH**, you can find settings to change the style of your mouse pointer and its size.

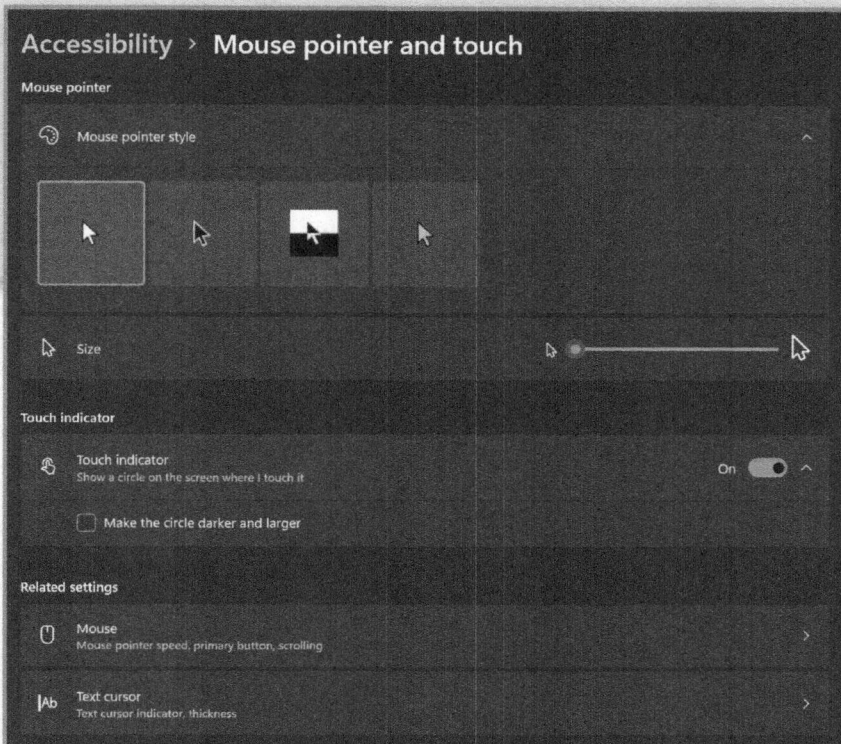

If you are using a touch screen device, you can also find settings to make the touch indicator larger and darker so that it is easier to see.

_ □ ✕

You can also adjust the pointer speed, known as **"mouse sensitivity."** This allows you to move your cursor across the screen faster, though it can also decrease precision.

To change your pointer speed, go to ⚙ **SETTINGS > BLUETOOTH & DEVICES > MOUSE** and move the slider to select the speed you want. In this menu you can also change your primary mouse button from left to right, and there are options for changing the scrolling settings using the wheel on your mouse. You can scroll multiple lines at once or set your mouse up so that rolling your wheel only scrolls down one line at a time.

_ □ ✕

COLOR FILTERS

Windows 11 offers a few different color filters so that people with color blindness or other vision problems can still see all the elements on their displays.

You can find these in ⚙ **SETTINGS > ACCESSIBILITY > COLOR FILTERS.**

You will see a color filter preview with a color wheel, an image and some color scales.

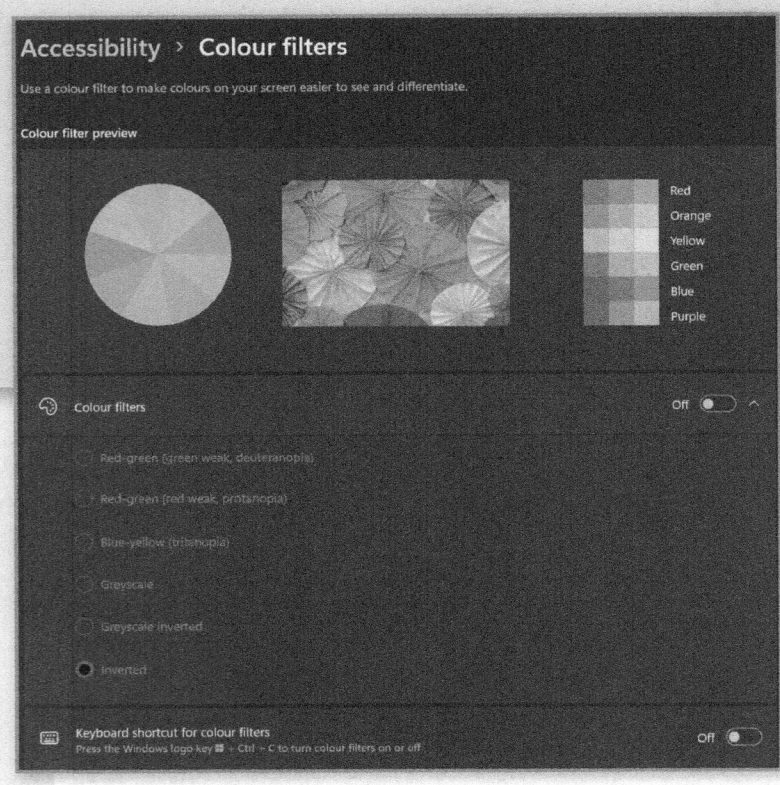

Windows 11 offers grayscale, inverted grayscale and an inverted color filter, as well as a red-green filter for people with weak green vision (deuteranopia), a red-green filter for people with weak red vision (protanopia) and a blue-yellow filter for people with **tritanopia**.

_ □ ✕

DEVICE USAGE

This is a new feature offered in Windows 11 to help and personalize your experience based on how you use your device.

In ⚙ **SETTINGS > PERSONALIZATION > DEVICE USAGE** you can find many different

21°C Sunny intervals   12:00 AM 01/01/2022

_ ☐ ✕

options which you can toggle on or off. This includes Gaming, Family, Creativity, School, Entertainment, and Business. You can choose to turn one or more of these features on and Windows 11 will then provide tips, ads, and other recommendations on services and tools to optimize your experience.

For example if you select Gaming, Windows 11 will be able to offer you Xbox Game Pass trials or suggest apps and games to try out.

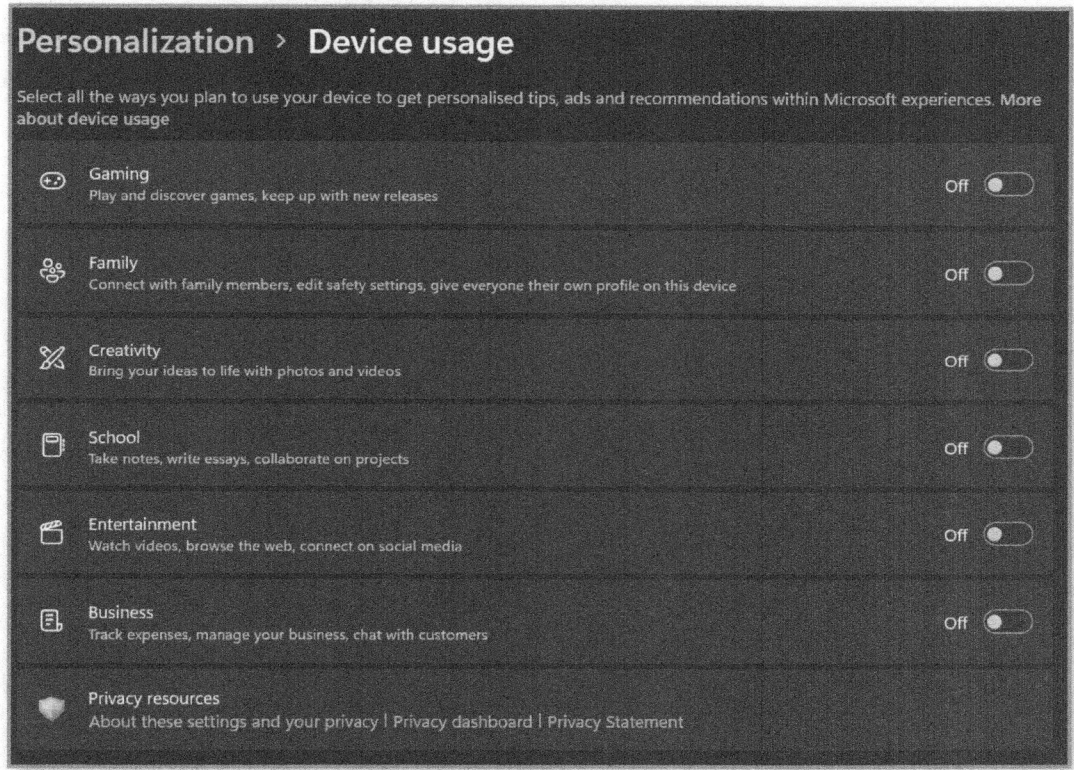

_ ☐ ✕

HOW TO PAIR BLUETOOTH DEVICES

If your computer or device is Bluetooth enabled, you can easily connect headphones, speakers, keyboards, mice and phones.

You can also get USB Bluetooth adapters which plug into a USB port if your device doesn't have Bluetooth functionality built in.

To pair (connect) a device with your computer using Bluetooth, first make sure that Bluetooth is turned on.

Visit **SETTINGS > BLUETOOTH & DEVICES** where you will find a toggle switch.

Next, **click on the Add device button** and your computer will begin to search for any nearby devices. Make sure that the device you are trying to pair is also turned on and in pairing mode. When your device shows up on screen, click on it to pair.

Alternatively, **you can click on your taskbar corner to bring up the Quick settings menu.** Here you will see a **Bluetooth button** which can be quickly turned on or off. Your computer will automatically pair with any devices that are in range which have already been paired in the past.

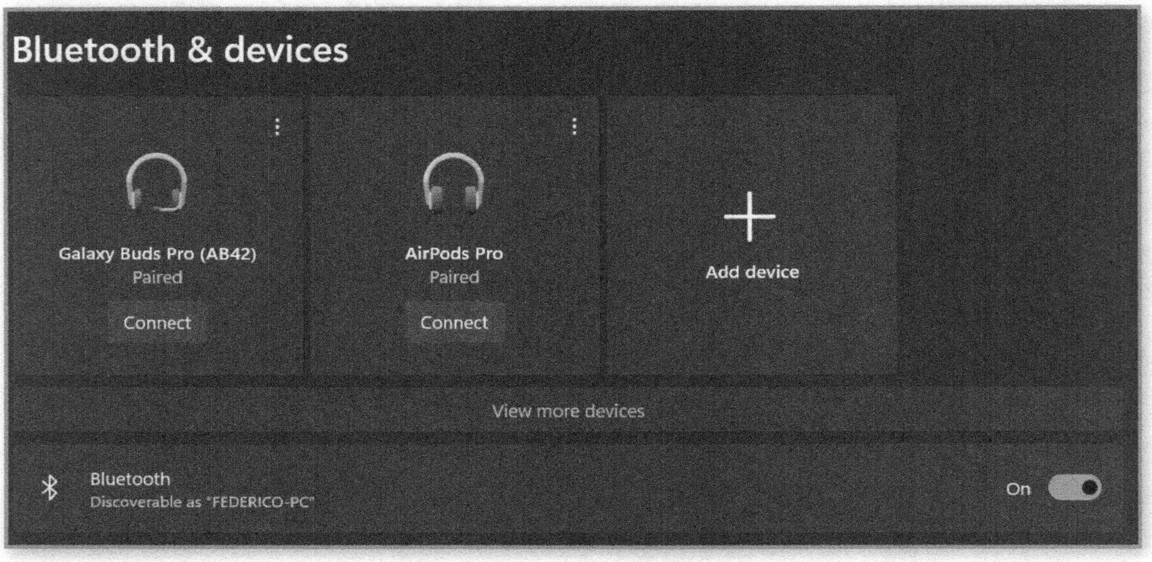

HOW TO INSTALL A SCANNER OR PRINTER

Windows 11 is good at automatically identifying any network or wireless printers and will make sure to download all of the drivers needed to properly run the equipment.

To add a new printer or scanner, begin by making sure it is powered up and plugged into the computer or network, or the wireless connection is turned on correctly.

_ □ ✕

Then visit ⚙ **SETTINGS > BLUETOOTH & DEVICES > PRINTERS & SCANNERS.**

Click the Refresh button so that Windows 11 can begin searching for the device. You should see the name of your printer or scanner appear in the list. Click on your printer or scanner and it will be installed and ready to use.

If you do not see your printer or scanner appear in the list, you will have to try another option. This may happen with older models. Click on "The printer that I want isn't listed" to add one manually. Follow the prompts on screen to connect the printer or scanner and install all the necessary drivers. If you have a wireless printer, you must ensure it is connected to the same network as your computer.

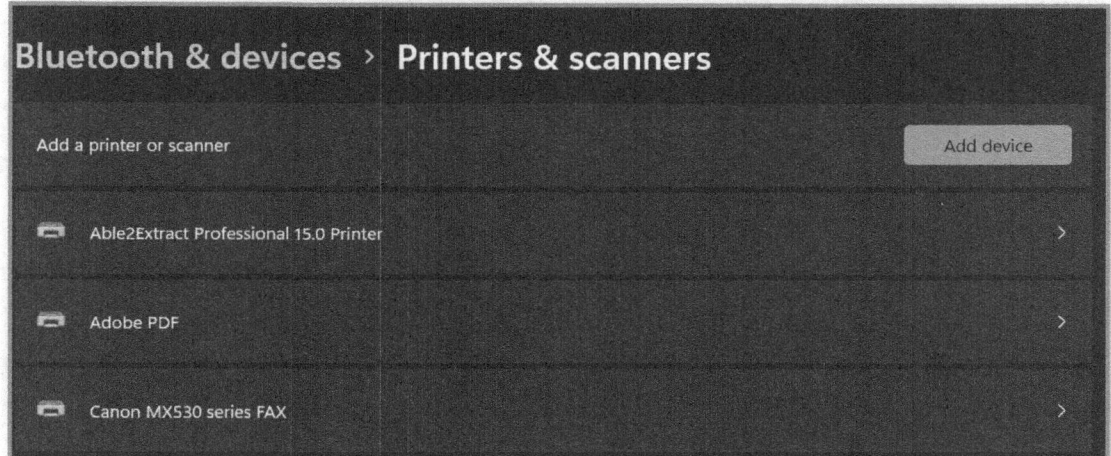

_ □ ✕

HOW TO LINK AN ANDROID SMARTPHONE TO YOUR COMPUTER

With Windows 11's "Your Phone" app it is easier than ever to stay connected. You can connect your Android phone to your computer so that you can easily sync photos, videos, messages, calls, notifications and more.

To link your Android phone to your computer, open the "Your Phone" app. You can do this through:

⚙ **SETTINGS > BLUETOOTH & DEVICES > YOUR PHONE > OPEN YOUR PHONE.**

_ □ ✕

Once the app is open, make sure you have your phone on hand, and click **"Get Started."** You may be asked to sign into your Microsoft account before moving on.

You will need to download the "Your Phone Companion" app onto your phone. This app is available on the Google app Play store or you can access it through **www.aka. ms/yourpc.**

Once the app has been installed, you can check the box that says, **"I have the Your Phone Companion - Link to Windows App ready,"** and then click the **"Pair with QR code" button**. You will see a QR code being displayed on your screen.

Open the "Your Phone Companion" on your Android phone and **select "Link your phone and PC"** and then 'Continue.'

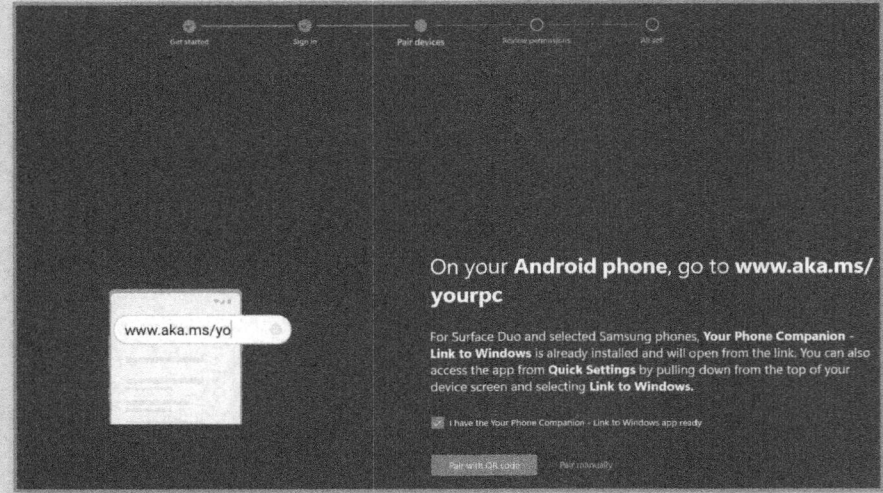

Your camera will open, point it to the computer screen so that the app can **scan the QR code**. Then press **'Done.'**

Your phone will now be linked to your computer. Press **'Continue.'**

You can now open the Your Phone app on your PC and get access to all the messages, notifications, media and call facilities on your smartphone.

If you are using a Samsung device, Windows 11 offers the ability to mirror your phone screen directly onto your computer. This means you can see a small window that looks exactly like your smartphone, and you can click on all your apps just like you would on your smartphone.

HOW TO PROJECT TO A WIRELESS DISPLAY

Wireless displays are used to seamlessly project your computer's screen onto a second display like a larger monitor or even some smart TVs. To enable this feature visit

21°C
Sunny intervals

12:00 AM
01/01/2022

— ☐ ✕

⚙ **SETTINGS > APPS > OPTIONAL FEATURES > ADD AN OPTIONAL FEATURE > VIEW FEATURES.**

You will see a search bar, type **"wireless display." Click on the checkbox to select this option, and then press Next**. Windows will download and install the relevant software after clicking Install.

You should not be able to see "Wireless display" in the Optional features menu in the Apps settings. You may need to reset your PC before these settings are properly integrated. Now you can set up your wireless projection by going to

⚙ **SETTINGS > SYSTEM > PROJECTING TO THIS PC**.

Look for the drop-down menu that says **"Always Off" and change this setting to "Available everywhere on secure networks"** or "Available everywhere". Next, click the link that says, **"Launch the Connect app to project to this PC."**

Now you can connect any device that is on the same network as your Windows 11 PC.

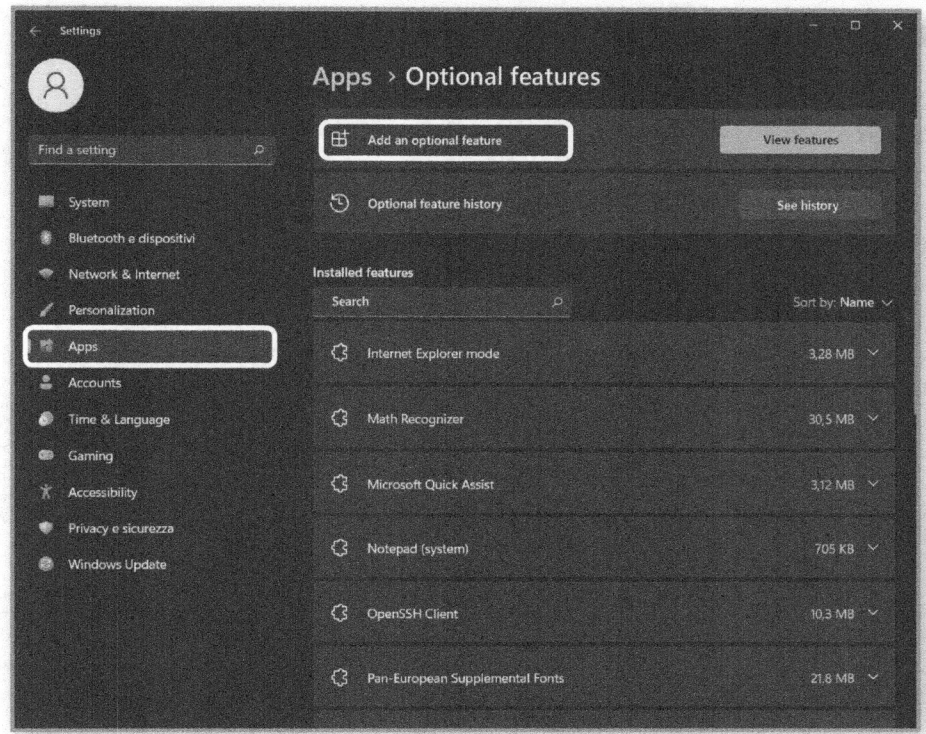

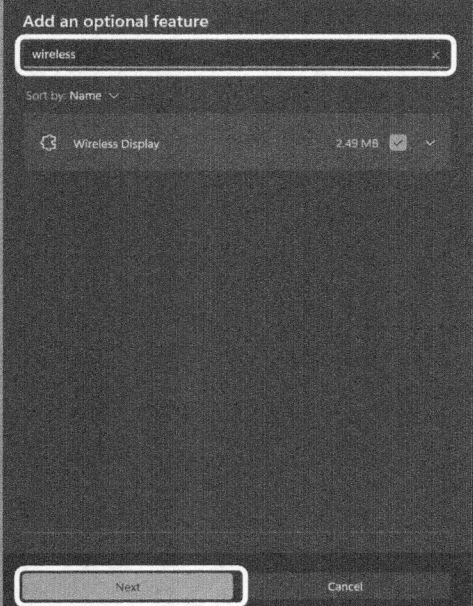

CHAPTER 3:

GETTING COMFORTABLE WITH DESKTOP

The Desktop is the starting point for everything you want to do on your computer. From your desktop, you can view the taskbar and Start menu, as well as any other desktop shortcuts, your wallpaper, and open windows. The Desktop can show you important information about the status of your computer using the taskbar corner.

🔍 HOW THE DESKTOP WORKS

HOW TO CHANGE THE DATE AND TIME

To set or adjust the time and date, you will need to right-click on the clock found on the right side of the taskbar corner.

You will see a small pop-up menu; click "Adjust date and time;" this will open up the Time and date settings in the ⚙**Settings app.** It is best to select **"Set time automatically,"** which will sync your computer with data collected online. Occasionally you will need to sync your computer to keep it updated.

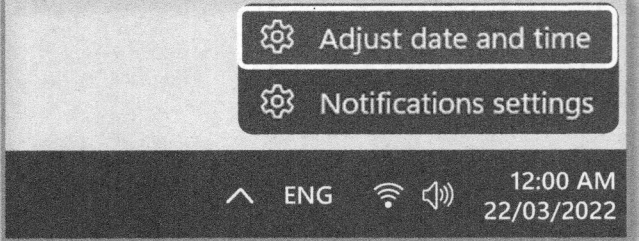

_ ☐ ✕

MOVING AND RESIZING WINDOWS

You can move around a window on your desktop by clicking and dragging the Title bar located at the very top of the window. Resizing a window is as easy as moving your cursor to the edges of the window, either on the sides of the bottom, where your pointer will change to a small icon showing double-sided arrows. When you see these double-sided arrows, click and then pull or push the edge of the window to stretch or shrink it to your desired size. You can also drag the corners of the window in the same way.

Another way to change the size of your windows is to click on the title bar and then drag the window to the top of your desktop. This will cause the window to automatically maximize, stretching to fit the entirety of your desktop. When a window is maximized, you can click on its title bar and drag it downward, which will shrink its size.

There are also three buttons (though sometimes four) on the right-hand side of a windows title bar, which can be used to resize windows. The first button is a horizontal line that you can click to minimize or maximize a window. Minimizing a window will remove it entirely from view. However, the app is still open and running, and you can click on the app icon in the taskbar to bring the window back into view.

Finally, **a new feature called Snap Windows has been added to Windows 11.** you can find this feature by hovering your cursor over the second button on the right-hand side of a window's title bar. This will bring up a small menu showing different layouts, including side-by-side and grids. You can move your mouse cursor over these layouts and select precisely how you want your active window to be arranged. You can enable or disable Snap Windows in

⚙ **SETTINGS > SYSTEM > MULTITASKING > SNAP WINDOWS.**

HOW TO TAKE A SCREENSHOT

Taking a screenshot involves capturing an image of your entire desktop and storing it on your computer's clipboard.

To do this, you simply need to press the PrtSc (Print Screen) button on your keyboard. Then you can open up any app that will accept an image, such as Microsoft Word, Adobe Photoshop, or Paint 3D, and paste your screenshot.

_ ☐ ✕

Paste the image by either right-clicking and selecting Paste or using the keyboard shortcut **Ctrl+V**. If you only want to capture an image of an active window, you can press **Alt+PrtSc** and follow the same steps.

You can also capture screenshots using the Windows 11 Snipping tool, which can be opened by searching **"Snipping Tool" in the Start menu.**

You will find three buttons at the app's top: New, Rectangle Mode, and No Delay. Click on Rectangle mode to show a drop-down menu with different capture modes:

- **Rectangle mode** allows you to use your mouse to draw a rectangle over the area you want to capture in an image.

- **Window mode** will take a screenshot of the active window.

- **Full-screen mode** will take a screenshot of your entire desktop.

- **Free-form mode** allows you to draw any shape with your mouse, and the content within will be captured in a screenshot.

The snipping tool offers 3, 5, and 10 seconds delay features.

When you have captured your screenshot, the Snipping Tool offers useful editing features such as cropping, drawing, highlighting, a ruler, eraser, and save.

There is another way to take a screenshot, use **Windows + Maiusc + S combination button.** You will be able to take a customize screenshot that will be showed on notification panel. Here you will be able to **save your print screen in a personalized folder**. You can also use **ctrl + c** and **ctrl + v** to copy and paste the screenshot after you took the screenshot.

OPENING A SECOND DESKTOP

You can create multiple desktops by using the Desktop icon ▨ **in your taskbar.** Hover your mouse cursor over the icon in the taskbar to reveal a small pop-up that shows your current desktop and an additional icon with a + symbol.

Click on the + symbol to create a new desktop. When you hover over the Desktop icon on your taskbar, you will see two small windows that you can easily switch between. You can add many desktops in this way. You can use these desktops to keep all of your tasks

21°C
Sunny intervals

12:00 AM
01/01/2022

_ □ ✕

separate. For example, windows for work can be kept on the first desktop, but you can place windows for entertainment on the second desktop.

You can move your windows onto these different desktops. Simply click on the Title bar of the window you want to move and drag it to the Desktop icon on the taskbar. You will see the small windows pop up. Drag the window to the Desktop you want to use and release your mouse button.

_ □ ✕

HOW TO QUICKLY SWITCH BETWEEN OPEN APPS

If you have multiple app windows open on your desktop you can easily cycle through these using the keyboard shortcut Alt+Tab. This will bring up an overlay screen showing each of your windows. Your current window will be highlighted.

To select a different app window, continue holding the Alt button while pressing the Tab button to cycle through the different windows. When you land on the one you are looking for, simply release the Alt and Tab buttons. You can also use your mouse and

_ □ ✕

click on different windows in this overlay screen.

Another way to view open windows is to press **Win+Tab.** This will bring up the Task View, showing each of your open apps. You can use your arrow keys to navigate to a different window and then press Enter to open up the selected app or click on it with your mouse.

_ □ ✕

🔍 HOW TO OPEN TASK MANAGER

Task Manager is a system monitor tool used to show tasks, processes, performance measures, and the overall health of your computer. You can use it to see how many resources an app is using, to close a frozen program, or prevent an app from opening upon Startup.

You can open Task Manager by:

- Pressing **Ctrl+Alt+Delete**
- Pressing **Ctrl+Shift+Esc**
- **Typing 'Task Manager'** in the Start menu.
- Pressing the **Windows+R keys** and then **typing 'taskmgr'** and then clicking **OK** or hitting the Enter key.

21°C
Sunny intervals

12:00 AM
01/01/2022

— ☐ ✕

In Task Manager, you will see a Navigation pane on the left showing Processes, Performance, App History, Startup apps, Users, Details, and Services:

- **Processes:** shows you how many resources your apps use, including CPU, GPU, memory, disk, and network usage.

- **Performance:** shows you real-time graphs of the resource usage statistics for different apps.

- **App history:** can be used to view how much network and CPU resources different Store apps have used.

- **Startup:** shows you a list of apps that will automatically open and start running when you turn on your computer and sign into your account.

- **Users:** shows how many resources are used by the different user accounts on your computer.

- **Details:** shows more in-depth information about your apps.

- **Services:** shows information about some of the background processes required to run your computer's apps.

Task Manager						
File Options View						
Processes Performance App history Startup Users Details Services						
			17%	71%	0%	0%
Name		Status	CPU	Memory	Disk	Network
Apps (7)						
> Firefox (10)			4.3%	1,424.9 MB	0.1 MB/s	0.1 Mbps
> Google Chrome (31)			0.6%	779.8 MB	0 MB/s	0 Mbps
> Microsoft Word			0.4%	183.4 MB	0 MB/s	0 Mbps
> Skype (7)			1.1%	320.7 MB	0.1 MB/s	0 Mbps
> Spotify (32 bit) (4)			0.2%	177.3 MB	0.1 MB/s	0 Mbps
> Task Manager			6.3%	35.4 MB	0.2 MB/s	0 Mbps
> Windows Explorer (2)			0.2%	77.5 MB	0 MB/s	0 Mbps

21°C
Sunny intervals

12:00 AM
01/01/2022

To close an unresponsive or frozen app, click on Processes and find the app in the list, click on it, and then press End Task in the lower right corner of the Task Manager. You can also **right-click and select "End task"** to force Windows 11 to close the app.

You will see a button that says "Fewer options" at the bottom left of the Task Manager. Clicking on this button will reduce the amount of information you see, showing only the active apps and excluding any background processes. You can select an app from this more simplified list and then click End Task in the bottom right of the window to shut it down.

To prevent an app from opening on Startup, which can cause your computer to become significantly slower, click on Startup apps and scroll through the list. Identify any programs that can be removed, right-click on them and select 'disable' to prevent them from opening upon startup of your computer. Make sure not to disable important Microsoft systems or hardware programs. You can identify these because Microsoft Corporation will be listed under Publisher.

CHAPTER 4:

HOW TO INSTALL ANY SOFTWARE

🔍 HOW TO INSTALL GOOGLE CHROME

Even though Windows 11 does offer its own internet browser called Edge, many users prefer to use Google Chrome for all their internet-based activities. **To download Google Chrome, you will need to use your edge browser.**

Type **google.com/chrome** into the address bar and hit enter. You can also type "Google Chrome" into the search bar and hit enter, then select the first result that comes up; this will direct you to a download page. Click the download button and then select Accept and Install.

Open File Explorer on your desktop, go to the Downloads library to find the installation package and double-click it to install Google Chrome. The installation process will ask you to create a desktop shortcut and an app icon in the taskbar. You can deselect these options if you don't want shortcuts.

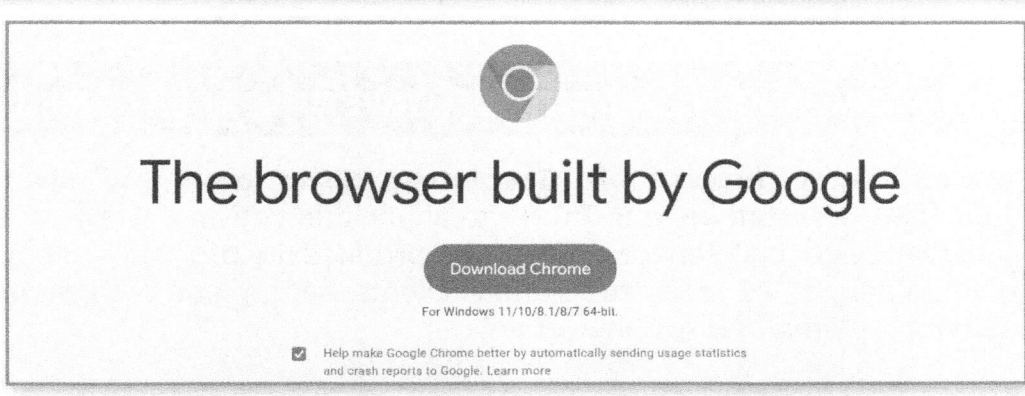

The browser built by Google

Download Chrome

For Windows 11/10/8.1/8/7 64-bit.

☑ Help make Google Chrome better by automatically sending usage statistics and crash reports to Google. Learn more

_ ▢ ✕

HOW TO MAKE GOOGLE CHROME YOUR DEFAULT BROWSER

Setting a default browser means that anytime you click on an internet link, that browser will be the one to open it. To set Google Chrome or any other browser as your default browser, you will need to go to:

⚙ **SETTINGS > SYSTEM > APPS > DEFAULT APPS.**

In the search bar, type **'Edge'** to show all the links and file types for which Edge is the default app. You must click on each of these links and file types and select Google Chrome as the default browser instead. Click **OK** to confirm your selection.

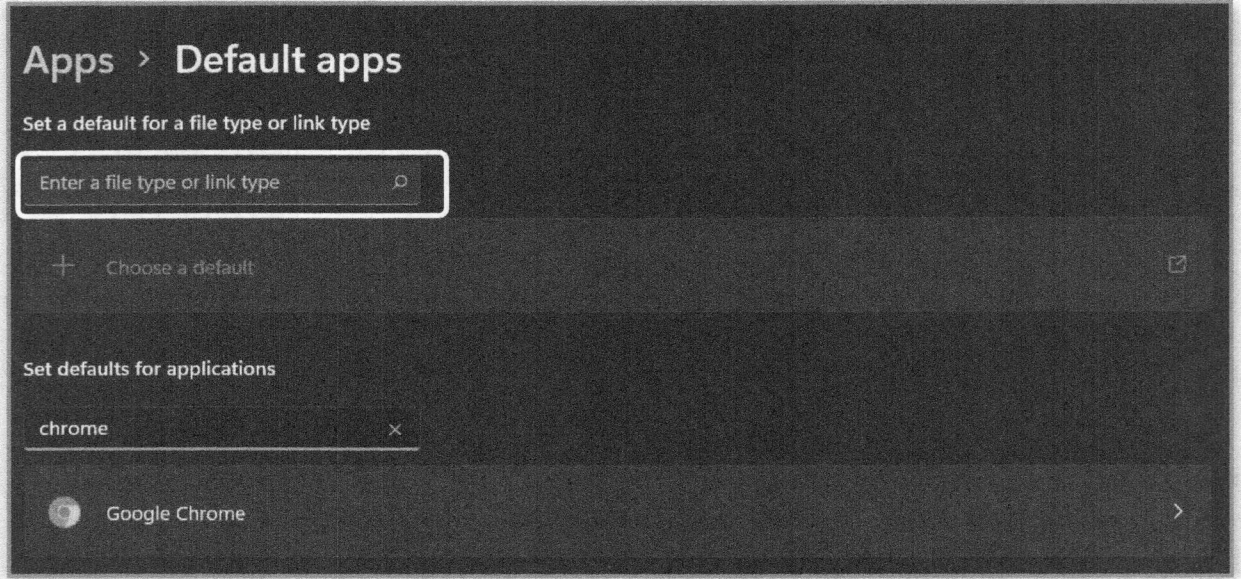

_ ▢ ✕

HOW TO DOWNLOAD AND INSTALL ANY SOFTWARE ONTO YOUR COMPUTER

You can use an internet browser like Google chrome to locate and download any software you want to install on your PC. This can include antivirus software, browsers, VPN (virtual private network) services, office, and productivity programs, media players, photo and video editors, PC repair tools, email clients, backup and recovery assistants, file management systems, and social programs.

21°C
Sunny intervals

12:00 AM
01/01/2022

These are some of the best and most trusted options available for each of these software types:

- **Antivirus**
  - ◊ Kaspersky Total Security
  - ◊ Norton 360 Deluxe
  - ◊ McAfee Internet Security

- **Browsers**
  - ◊ Google Chrome
  - ◊ Microsoft Edge
  - ◊ Mozilla Firefox

- **VPN services**
  - ◊ ExpressVPN
  - ◊ NordVPN
  - ◊ Surfshark

- **Productivity/office**
  - ◊ Microsoft 365
  - ◊ Google workspace
  - ◊ Apache Open Office

- **Media players**
  - ◊ VLC Media Player
  - ◊ GOM Player
  - ◊ 5KPlayer

- **Photo and video editors**
  - ◊ Adobe Suite
  - ◊ CorelDRAW
  - ◊ Clip Studio Paint

- **PC repair tools**
  - ◊ System Mechanic Ultimate Defense
  - ◊ Restore
  - ◊ Outbyte PC Repair

- **Email clients**
  - ◊ Microsoft Outlook
  - ◊ eM Client
  - ◊ Thunderbird

- **Backup and recovery**
  - ◊ Acronis True Image
  - ◊ EaseUS Todo Backup
  - ◊ Paragon Backup & Recovery

- **File management**
  - ◊ Total Commander
  - ◊ Directory Opus
  - ◊ File Viewer Plus

- **Social**
  - ◊ Zoom
  - ◊ WhatsApp
  - ◊ Skype
  - ◊ Facebook Messenger

You can find the software you are looking for by typing in the name and 'download' into your browser search bar. Make sure to click the link that takes you to the software developer's own trusted website. You will need to purchase many programs before downloading and installing them, including Microsoft Office 365 and various Adobe products. Once you have completed the payment process, you will be redirected to a download link with steps detailing how to install the software properly.

Ensure that your computer meets the minimum system requirements for the software you want to download. This information should be available on the website. Next, find the download link and accept any required terms and conditions. When the file is downloaded, you can begin the installation process. Most programs will come with installation guides to assist you, and you will only need to check some boxes and click Next, Accept, or Install.

HOW TO INSTALL VLC MEDIA PLAYER

VLC is one of the most highly-regarded, free, and open-source media players available. You can use VLC to play downloaded videos, DVDs, audio files, and almost any other kind of media file. To download VLC, visit **videolan.org/vlc/index.html** using your browser.

Click the large orange button that says, **"Download VLC."** If the installation does not begin automatically, find the file in your Downloads, and double click. A window will come up that says, **"Do you want to allow this app to make changes to your device?"** Click **Yes**, and then select a language and installation location before VLC can complete the installation. **You can now open up the VLC app using your Start menu**.

— ☐ ✕

HOW TO INSTALL KASPERSKY INTERNET SECURITY

Though **Windows 11 is one of the most secure operating systems ever released by Microsoft**, you can still benefit from **using antivirus** and internet security software such as Kaspersky.

Like most programs, Kaspersky has a set of system requirements that your computer must meet:

- 1 GB of memory (RAM)
- 600 MB of free disk space to download the application
- 1.3 GB of free disk space to install the application
- Internet connection

You will need to purchase a license for this software by visiting **https://www.kaspersky.co.za/downloads#compare-table** in your browser. Sign up for a My Kaspersky account and then follow the instructions to download and install the latest version. Click on the installation file in your Downloads library and follow the prompts.

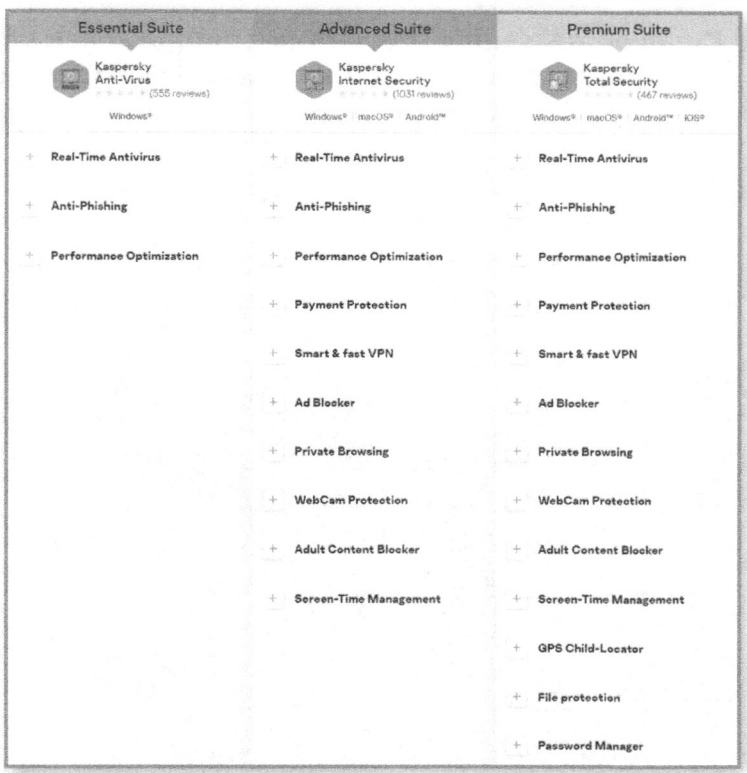

Essential Suite	Advanced Suite	Premium Suite
Kaspersky Anti-Virus (555 reviews) Windows®	Kaspersky Internet Security (1031 reviews) Windows® macOS® Android™	Kaspersky Total Security (467 reviews) Windows® macOS® Android™ iOS®
Real-Time Antivirus	Real-Time Antivirus	Real-Time Antivirus
Anti-Phishing	Anti-Phishing	Anti-Phishing
Performance Optimization	Performance Optimization	Performance Optimization
	Payment Protection	Payment Protection
	Smart & fast VPN	Smart & fast VPN
	Ad Blocker	Ad Blocker
	Private Browsing	Private Browsing
	WebCam Protection	WebCam Protection
	Adult Content Blocker	Adult Content Blocker
	Screen-Time Management	Screen-Time Management
		GPS Child-Locator
		File protection
		Password Manager

kaspersky

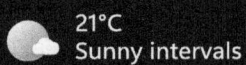   

_ □ ✕

The installer will look for any updates online and then proceed to the terms and conditions, which you must accept by clicking the checkbox. Next, Kaspersky will be installed.

When the window that says, **"Do you want to allow this app to make changes to your device?"** pops up, **click 'Yes.'** Kaspersky will show you a window with several recommended settings when the installation is complete, which you can select or deselect before clicking Apply.

When you run the program for the first time, it will ask you for an activation code. This is a unique combination of letters and numbers in the format xxxxx-xxxxx-xxxxx-xxxxx. This code entitles you to use the software and proves that you legally purchased it.

You will be asked for an activation code when using many different programs besides Kaspersky. You can find your unique activation code in an email that will be sent to you upon completing your purchase. **If you have installed the software from a boxed version, you will find the code inside the manual or retail box containing the CD.**

HOW TO INSTALL WHATSAPP MESSENGER

WhatsApp is one of the best messaging apps for keeping in touch with friends and family, and a desktop version will sync with the version on your smartphone so you can always see your chats.

Open the Microsoft Store 🔲 on your taskbar or type it into the Start menu ⬛. In the Microsoft Store, **type 'WhatsApp'** into the search bar and click on the result that says "WhatsApp Desktop." **You will see a 'Free' button**; click on this to download the app. That's it. Once the download and installation are complete, the app will be ready to run.

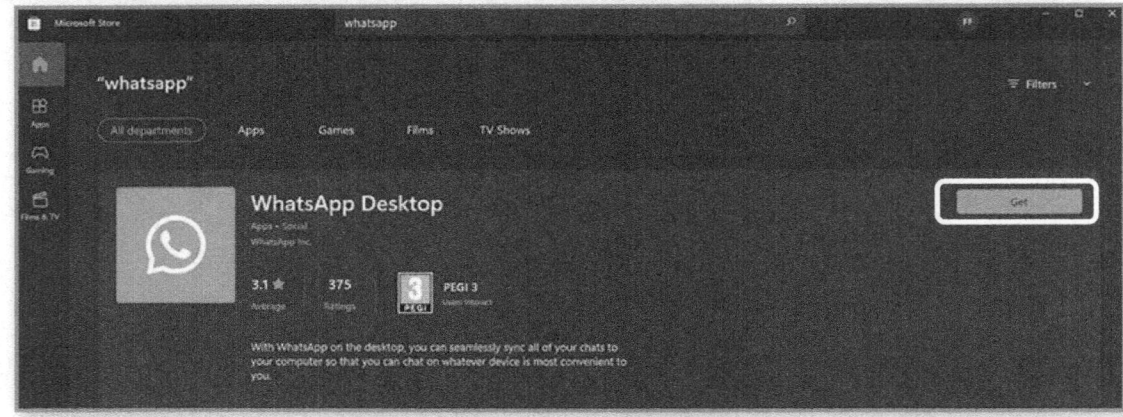

21°C
Sunny intervals

12:00 AM
01/01/2022

_ □ ✕

HOW TO INSTALL ZOOM

Zoom is a video chat service that allows you to speak with friends and family. It is one of many similar programs but is rated as one of the most efficient and easy to use.

Visit **zoom.us/download** and click the Download button. Click on the installation file in your Downloads folder and make sure to select yes when asked, "Do you want to allow this app to make changes to your device?" Zoom will be installed, and you can begin using it after a simple setup.

THINGS TO KEEP IN MIND

Windows 11 will always ask you if you want to allow the software to make changes to your device when installing new software. Make sure only to proceed if the software has been verified and is trusted.

You can determine how trustworthy a program is by searching the internet for some reviews beforehand. It is also critical to read through all the requested permissions when installing new software and do not agree to any unnecessary terms or conditions.

Some programs may ask for permission to access or change your privacy settings, pictures, and videos or complete network access when they do not need this information to run correctly. For example, a calendar app does not need access to your media. Make sure to uncheck these boxes before proceeding.

CHAPTER 5:

HOW TO NAVIGATE ON THE WEB WITH WINDOWS 11

Navigating the web is easy with a modern internet browser like Microsoft Edge or Google Chrome. This chapter will look at how to carry out some of the most important functions using both of these browsers, though you will find that they are very similar.

HOW TO USE A WEB BROWSER

Browsers come with many buttons and features to improve your internet browsing experience. (I menu in genere, nel minor spazio possibile)

NAVIGATING MICROSOFT EDGE

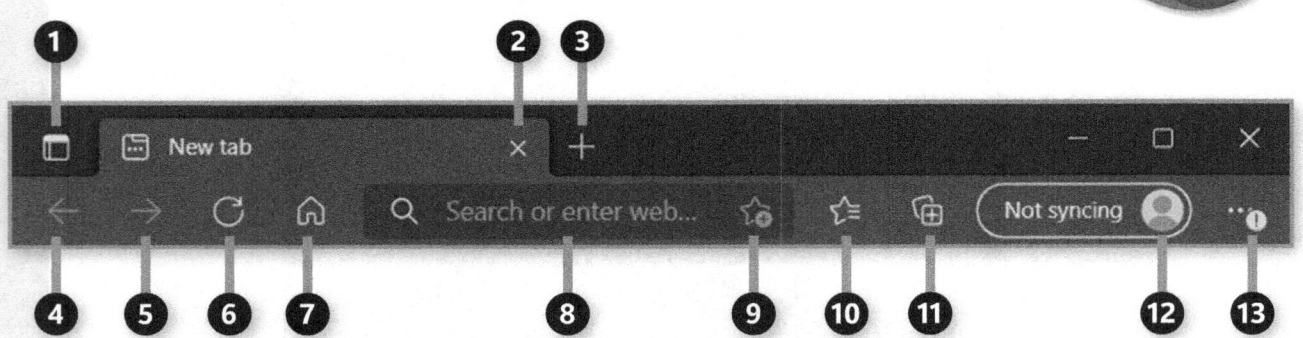

1. Tab actions menu - access tab options like viewing recently closed tabs.

2. Close this tab

3. Open a new tab

4. Go back

5. Go forward

6. Refresh the page

7. Go to home page

8. Address bar - where you can enter search terms or URLs

9. Add this page to your favorites

10. See your favorites

11. Add to a collection - use this feature to create reading lists that you can come back to at a later time

12. User profile - access your account and profile information

13. More tools

NAVIGATING GOOGLE CHROME

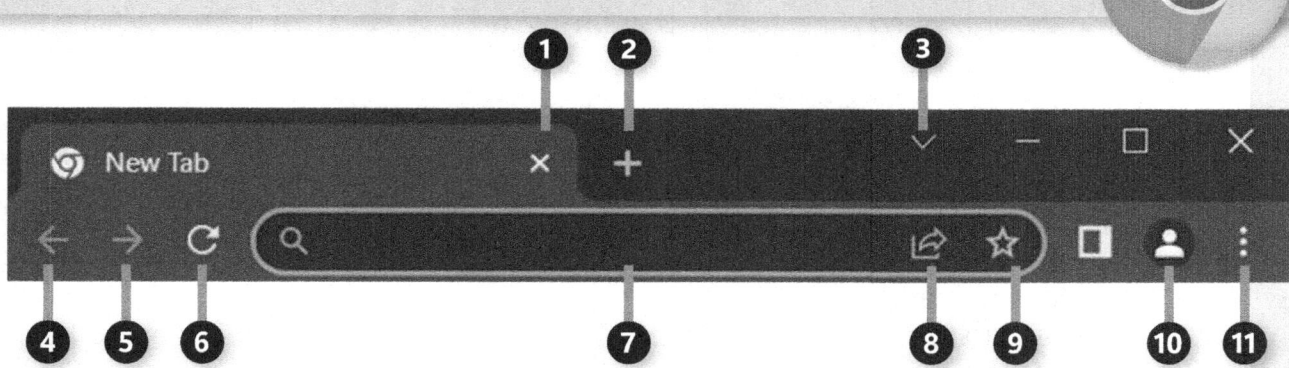

1. Close current tab

2. Open a new tab

3. View list of open and closed tabs

4. Go back

5. Go forward

6. Refresh the page

7. Address bar - where you can enter search terms or URLs

8. Share this page - click here to generate a link, send the page to one of your connected devices, create a QR code, or save the page as an HTML file.

9. Bookmark the current page

10. User profile - see your account and profile information

11. More tools

_ □ ✕

WHAT ARE TABS?

Internet browsers use a feature called Tabs so that you can open multiple web pages within the same window. Tabs can help to keep your desktop from becoming cluttered.

Tabs are shown at the very top of your browser, above the address bar. You can easily open a new tab by clicking the + symbol to the right of your current tab.

You can open any link in a new tab by right-clicking and selecting "Open in new tab." You can also open a link in a completely **new window by right-clicking and selecting "Open in new window."**

HOW TO ADD A BOOKMARK

A bookmark is a way to save and store a website's URL so that you can come back to it in the future.

- **Microsoft Edge**

    1. Visit the **website URL** you want to save.
    2. Click the **Star button** on the right-hand side of the toolbar.
    3. Click the **Star button with the + sign** to add a 'Favorite.'
    4. You will see the name of your website appear.
    5. Hit **Enter** to save.
    6. You can customize the website's name or add folders and subfolders to keep your Favorites organized.
    7. You can also use the keyboard shortcut **Ctrl+D** to add a website to your Favorites quickly.

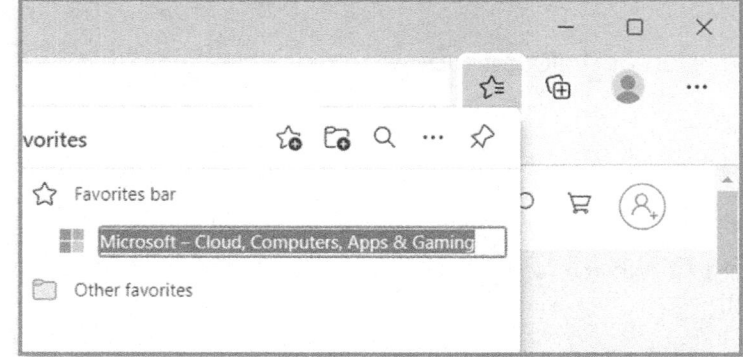

21°C
Sunny intervals

12:00 AM
01/01/2022

_ ☐ ✕

- **Google Chrome**

1. Visit the **website URL** you want to save.
2. Click the **Star button** on the right-hand side of the toolbar.
3. You will see the name of your website appear and the folder.
4. Hit **Enter** to save.
5. You can customize the web site's name or add folders and subfolders to keep your Bookmarks organized.
6. You can also use the keyboard shortcut **Ctrl+D** to add a website to your Bookmarks quickly.

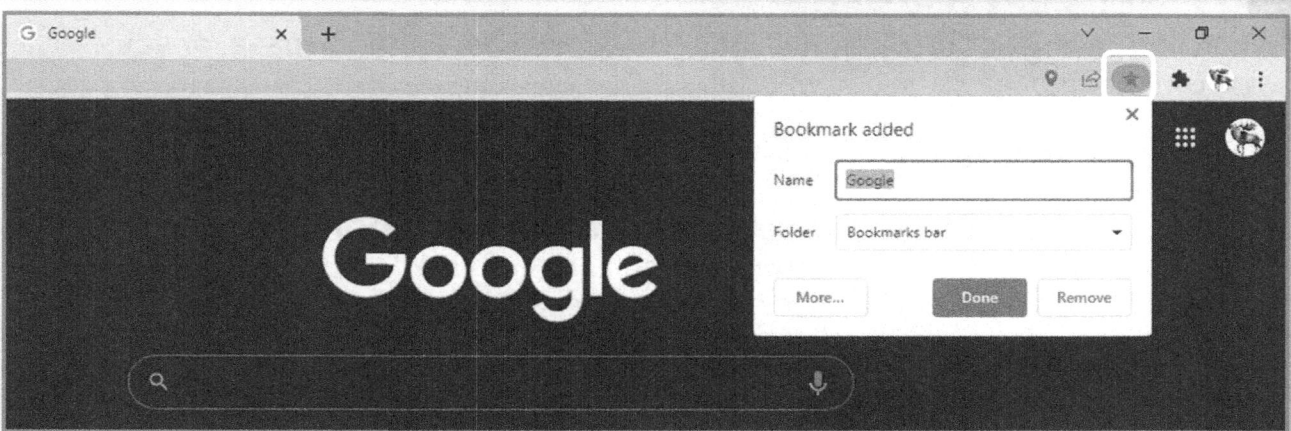

_ ☐ ✕

HOW TO SHOW THE BOOKMARKS BAR

You can display all of your bookmarks and bookmark folders in a bar at the top of your browser.

- **Microsoft Edge**

1. Click the **Tools button**, select: **SETTINGS > APPEARANCE > CUSTOMIZE THE TOOLBAR > SHOW FAVORITES BAR.**

2. Select 'Always' or "Only on new tabs" to display the favorites bar.
3. You can also use the keyboard shortcut **Ctrl + Shift + B** to hide or show the Favorites bar quickly.

_ □ ✕

- **Google Chrome**

   1. Click the Tools button, select

   SETTINGS > APPEARANCE > SHOW BOOKMARKS BAR.

   2. Toggle this to display the bookmarks bar.
   3. You can also use the keyboard shortcut **Ctrl + Shift + B** to hide or show the bookmarks bar quickly.

HOW TO SET A NEW HOMEPAGE

When you open your browser, it will direct you to a default homepage, or you can set your own homepage to be any website.

- **Microsoft Edge**

   1. Go to **SETTINGS > APPEARANCE > CUSTOMIZE TOOLBAR.**
   2. Toggle the **"Home button"** option and then click **"Set button URL."**
   3. This will direct you to the homepage settings, where you can set your homepage button to refer you to a new tab or a specific URL.

- **Google Chrome**

   1. Go to **SETTINGS > APPEARANCE.**
   2. Toggle the button for **"Show Home button"** to **'on.'**
   3. Choose whether to set your homepage to a New Tab Page or a specific URL.

VIEW AND DELETE YOUR BROWSING HISTORY

Your internet browser records all the web pages you have visited recently. You can easily view this information, clear all the records, or delete specific records.

- **Microsoft Edge**

   1. Click the **Tools button**, then select **History.**
   2. You will see some of the web pages you have visited in the last 90 days in a small window.
   3. You can delete individual records by hovering over them and clicking the **X**

21°C
Sunny intervals

12:00 AM
01/01/2022

that appears on the right-hand side.

4.   To clear all your browsing history, click on the three horizontal dots at the top of the History window and select "Clear browsing data."

5.   You can also open your browser history by pressing **Ctrl+H.**

6.   To see more detailed information such as the date and time when you visited your web pages, select **"Open history page"** after clicking the **three horizontal dots** at the top of the History window.

- **Google Chrome**

1.   Click the **Tools button**, then select **History**.

2.   You will see some of the web pages you have visited in the last 90 days in a small window.

3.   You can open one of these pages by clicking on it.

4.   To delete your search history, open the History tab or press **Ctrl+H.**

5.   You can select and deselect individual records using the checkboxes and then press the Delete button in the top right corner.

6.   You can **delete all your browser history** using the **"Clear browsing data"** button on the left side of the page.

HOW TO ENABLE PRIVATE BROWSING

When you use private browsing, your activity and data, such as search history, will not be stored on your device or your account. Keep in mind that these modes will not hide your browsing data from your internet service provider, who will still be able to see your network activity.

- **Microsoft Edge - InPrivate browsing**

1.   To open a new tab using InPrivate, **click on the three horizontal dots** in the top right of your window.

2.   Select '**New InPrivate Window.**

3.   You can also open an InPrivate window using the keyboard shortcut **Ctrl+Shift+N.**

- **Google Chrome - Incognito Mode**

    1. To open a new tab using Incognito mode, **click on the three vertical dots** in the top right of your window.
    2. Select **"New Incognito window."**
    3. You can also open an Incognito window using the keyboard shortcut Ctrl + **Shift + N.**

HOW TO ZOOM IN ON A PAGE

- **Microsoft Edge**

    1. **Click on the three horizontal dots** in the top right of your browser window.
    2. Navigate to '**Zoom**' and press + or - to zoom in or out.
    3. You can also hold the Ctrl button while using the wheel on your mouse to zoom in or out.

- **Google Chrome**

    1. **Click on the three vertical dots** in the top right of your browser window.
    2. Navigate to '**Zoom**' and press + or - to zoom in or out.
    3. You can also hold the Ctrl button while using the wheel on your mouse to zoom in or out.

HOW TO BLOCK ADS ON YOUR WEB BROWSER

Many websites display intrusive and distracting ads that pop up in your browser. You can use your internet browser to block some of these ads.

- **Microsoft Edge**

    1. Click on the **Tools button**, then select

    SETTINGS > COOKIES AND SITE PERMISSIONS > POP-UPS AND REDIRECTS.

    2. Make sure **to turn this setting on**.
    3. You can also customize these settings and add or block certain websites from showing pop-ups or redirecting you to another page.

21°C
Sunny intervals

12:00 AM
01/01/2022

_ □ ✕

- **Google Chrome**

    1. Click on the **Tools Button**, then select

    SETTINGS > SECURITY AND PRIVACY > SITE SETTINGS > POP-UPS AND REDIRECTS.

    2. Under **"Default behavior,"** ensure that you select the **"Don't allow sites to send pop-ups or use redirects"** option.
    3. You can also customize these settings to allow pop-ups from specific websites or ban pop-ups from certain websites by inputting their URLs.

RIGHT-CLICKING AN IMAGE OR LINK IN YOUR BROWSER

When you right-click an image or link in your internet browser, you will see a menu with many different options that can help to improve your productivity.

- **Microsoft Edge**

    ♦ **Open image/link in new tab** - opens the image/link in a new tab with the image/link URL in the address bar.

    ♦ **Save image/link as** - opens your File Explorer so that you can name and choose a location on your PC in which to save the image/link. Web pages are saved as HTML files.

    ♦ **Copy image/link** - places a copy of the image/link onto your clipboard so that you can paste it into another application.

    ♦ **Copy image link** - saves the image's URL to your clipboard.

    ♦ **Create QR Code for this image** - generates a unique QR code that links to the image URL, which you can scan using your phone camera.

    ♦ **Search the web for image** - search the web for similar images.

    ♦ **Search Bing in sidebar for image** - opens a sidebar with the Bing search engine to find similar images.

— □ ✕

♦ **Open in Immersive Reader** - opens your web page with a more refined layout that removes clutter and improves the reading experience.

♦ **Share** - allows you to share the web page through email, Facebook, or other social media.

♦ **Web select and Web capture** - a clipping tool to save screenshots.

♦ **Inspect** - view the web page's source code.

▢ Open link in new tab	
▭ Open link in new window	
▣ Open link in InPrivate window	
▦ Create QR Code for this image	
⊑▢ Send link to your devices	›
Save link as	
⊖ Copy link	
▤ Open image in new tab	
▨ Save image as	
▧ Copy image	
Copy image link	
▨ Search the web for image	
▨ Search in sidebar for image	
▤ Add to Collections	›
▨ Share	
▢ Web select	Ctrl+Shift+X
▨ Web capture	Ctrl+Shift+S
▢ Inspect	

— □ ✕

- **Google Chrome**

♦ **Open image/link in new tab** - opens the image/link in a new tab with the image URL in the address bar.

♦ **Save image/link as** - opens your File Explorer so that you can name and choose a location on your PC in which to save the image/link. Web pages are saved as HTML files.

♦ **Copy image/link** - places a copy of the image/link onto your clipboard so that you can paste it into another application.

21°C
Sunny intervals

12:00 AM
01/01/2022

◆   **Copy image address** - saves the image's URL to your clipboard.

◆   **Create QR Code for this image** - generates a unique QR code that links to the image URL, which you can scan using your phone camera.

◆   **Search image with Google Lens** - searches the web for images that are similar.

◆   **Inspect** - view the web page's source code.

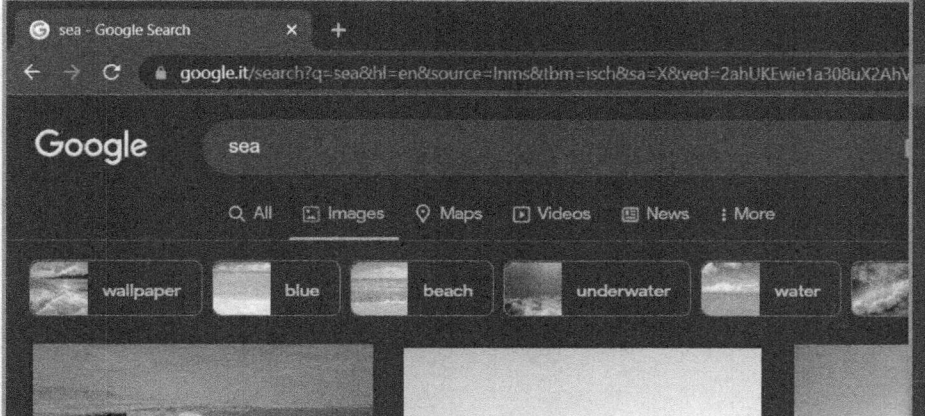
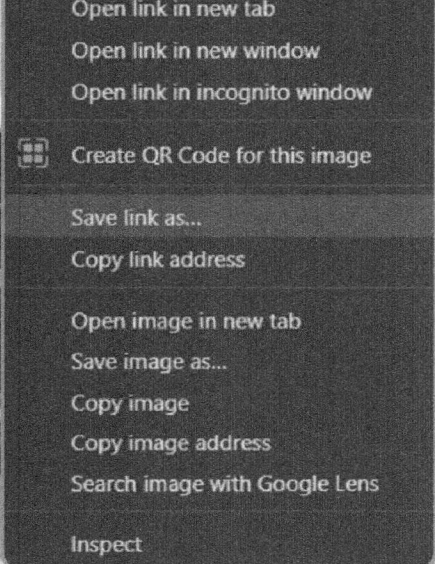

HOW TO DOWNLOAD A FILE

When browsing the web, you may want to download content such as a document or an image. Documents are often offered for download using a link.

You can download these links onto your computer by **right-clicking** and selecting the **"Save link as..."** option. This will open up your File Explorer so that you can name your download and choose the location in which you want the file to be saved.

Similarly, you can save almost any image found online by right-clicking, selecting **"Save image as...,"** naming the image, and choosing a location in which to save it.

_ ▢ ✕

ADD-ONS AND EXTENSIONS

Internet browsers offer simple tools to improve and customize your browsing experience. These tools will appear as small icons to the right of your address bar.

- **Microsoft Edge**

   ♦ You can find add-ons by **clicking the Tools button** and **selecting extensions.** This is also where you will go to manage your installed extensions.

   ♦ You will be redirected to the Edge Add-ons page, where you can browse through many kinds of tools suited for different purposes, including accessibility, blogging, communication, developer tools, entertainment, news & weather, photos, productivity, search tools, shopping, social, and sports. On this page, you can also find some of the featured apps in Most popular, Newest, Editor's picks, By Microsoft, Trending, and more.

   ♦ To install an add-on to your web browser, click the Get button, then select Add Extension on the pop-up window. This will add a button for the extension on the side of your address bar, and you may be redirected to the add-on's developer web page.

   ♦ To use the add-on, click on the small icon next to the address bar, and navigate through the various features offered in the menu.

   ♦ Make sure to check the ratings provided for all of the add-ons, as some may be faulty or not work properly.

- **Google Chrome**

   ♦ You can find extensions for Chrome at **chrome.google.com/webstore/category/extensions.** You can manage your existing extensions by clicking

TOOLS > MORE TOOLS > EXTENSIONS.

   ♦ The link will take you to the Google Web Store, where you can browse through thousands of extensions for different purposes, including accessibility, blogging, developer tools, fun, news & weather, photos, productivity, search tools, shopping, social and communication, and sports. The Web Store will also show

21°C
Sunny intervals

12:00 AM
01/01/2022

you some featured apps in different categories such as Recommended for you, Favorites of 2021, Extensions starter kit, Travel smarter, and more.

♦   To install an extension, click on it, select **"Add to Chrome,"** then select **Add Extension** on the pop-up window.

♦   You should now see a new icon next to your address bar, which you can click on to access the extension's features.

♦   If you do not see a new icon, you should see an icon of a puzzle piece which you can click to show all of your extensions. You can use the pin buttons to pin or unpin the extension icons to your taskbar so that you can always see them.

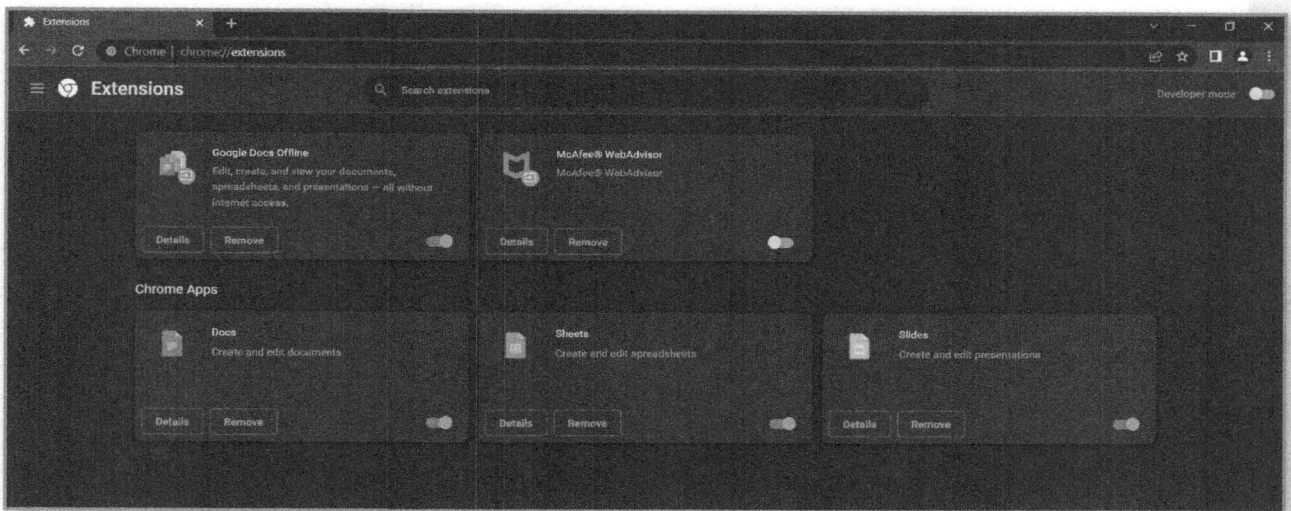

chrome://extensions

CHAPTER 6:

EMAILING WITH FAMILY AND FRIENDS

Email has come a long way from its humble beginnings, and there are many ways for you to access your mail using apps or your web browser. Use the Mail app or other email clients to send and receive messages instantly.

🔍 THE WINDOWS 11 MAIL APP

SETTING UP A NEW EMAIL ACCOUNT

- Open the **Mail app** ✉ using the **Start menu** ⊞.

- **If you are using the app for the first time, select Add account.**

    ◊ **If you have used the app before, you will need to go to Settings at the bottom of the navigation pane on the left, then select Manage Accounts.**

- Choose what kind of account you would like to set up. You can choose to use an existing Outlook account or create a new one. You can also use an Office 365, Google, Yahoo, or iCloud account. Alternatively, you can use other types of email accounts that use POP or IMAP, but this will require advanced setup options.

    ◊ If you choose a Google account and have enabled two-step verification (recommended), you will need to enter your unique 2-step verification code sent to your email or phone number.

21°C
Sunny intervals

12:00 AM
01/01/2022

- Enter the information required for sign-in, including the email address and password.

- Select **Done**, and your account will begin syncing. The mail app will download all of your email and contacts for you.

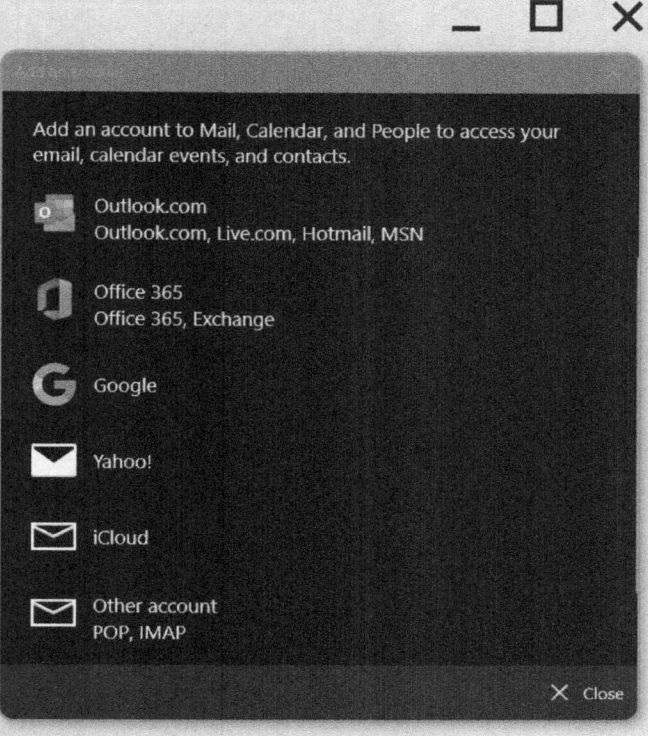

ADVANCED SETUP

Older types of email accounts may require advanced setup options. Select Advanced options when prompted, and then input the necessary information.

ADDING MULTIPLE EMAIL ACCOUNTS

The Mail app does not limit you to a single email address, and you can add multiple different accounts.

- To add a second or third account, **open the Mail app.**

- In the navigation pane, click:
SETTINGS > MANAGE ACCOUNTS > + ADD ACCOUNT.

- Choose what email account you would like to add from the list.

- Configure your account using the same steps as mentioned previously.

- You can access mail from different accounts by selecting your account from the navigation pane.

- **When composing new emails, make sure you send them from the correct email account.** You can click on your desired email address in the navigation pane to switch accounts.

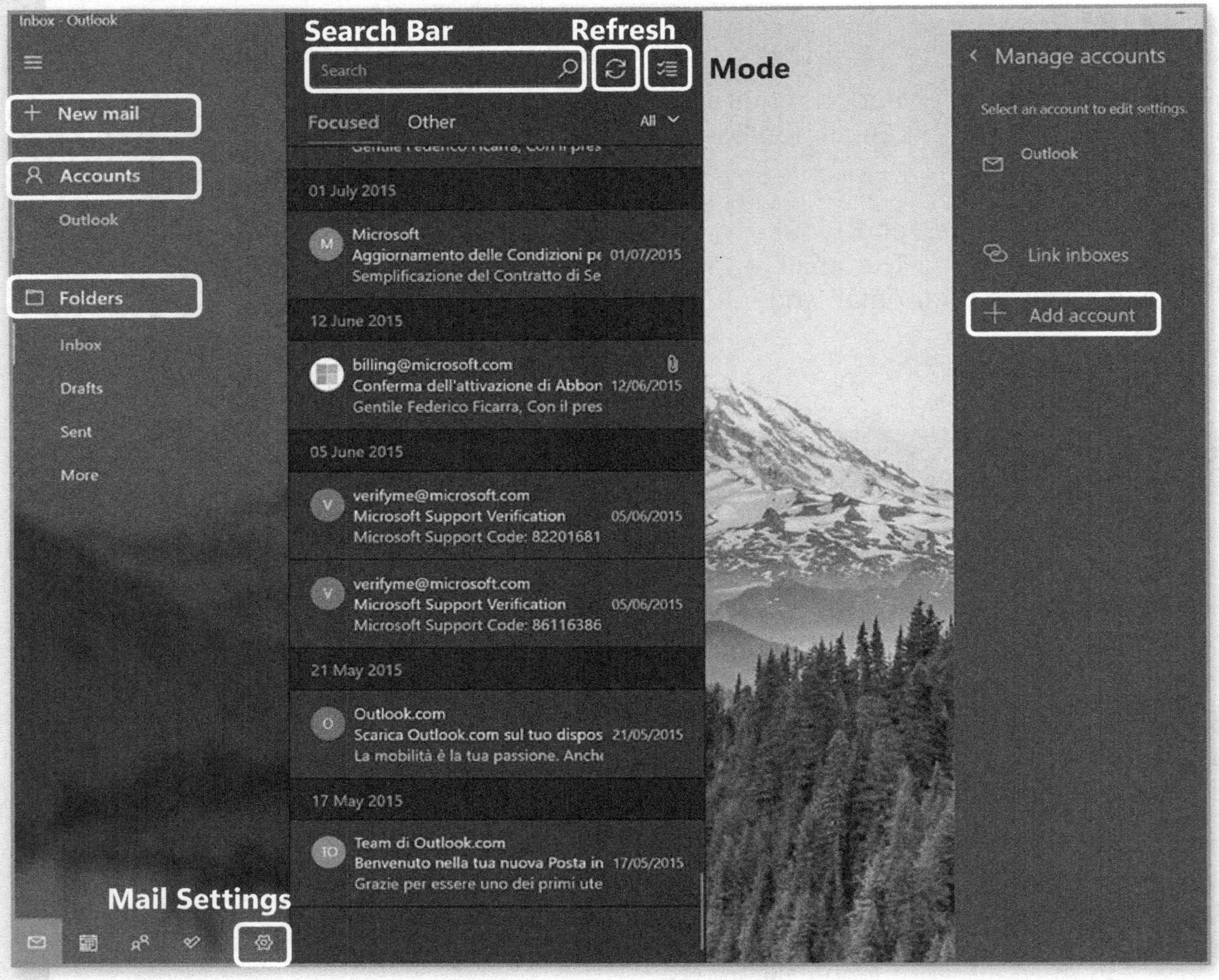

Inbox - Outlook

Search Bar　　　**Refresh**

Search 🔍 ⟳ ☰　**Mode**

< Manage accounts

Select an account to edit settings.

✉ Outlook

+ **New mail**

👤 **Accounts**

Outlook

📁 **Folders**

Focused　　Other　　　All ⌄

Gentile Federico Ficarra, Con il pres

01 July 2015

Ⓜ Microsoft
Aggiornamento delle Condizioni pe 01/07/2015
Semplificazione del Contratto di Se

12 June 2015

⊞ billing@microsoft.com 📎
Conferma dell'attivazione di Abbon 12/06/2015
Gentile Federico Ficarra, Con il pres

Inbox

Drafts

Sent

More

05 June 2015

Ⓥ verifyme@microsoft.com
Microsoft Support Verification 05/06/2015
Microsoft Support Code: 82201681

Ⓥ verifyme@microsoft.com
Microsoft Support Verification 05/06/2015
Microsoft Support Code: 86116386

21 May 2015

Ⓞ Outlook.com
Scarica Outlook.com sul tuo dispos 21/05/2015
La mobilità è la tua passione. Anch

17 May 2015

TO Team di Outlook.com
Benvenuto nella tua nuova Posta in 17/05/2015
Grazie per essere uno dei primi ute

🔗 Link inboxes

+ Add account

Mail Settings

✉ 📅 👥 ✏ ⚙

＿ □ ✕

USING THE MAIL APP

In the navigation pane on the left side of the **Mail App**, you will see several buttons.

- **Collapse** - collapses the navigation pane to reduce clutter.
- **+ New mail** - compose a new email.
- **Accounts** - View your account information.
- **Folders** - includes your Inbox, Drafts, Sent, and Archive folders.
- **Switch to Mail** - Used to toggle between the Mail and Calendar apps.
- **Switch to Calendar** - used to toggle between the Mail and Calendar apps.
- **Settings** - access the Mail App settings.

21°C
Sunny intervals

 12:00 AM
01/01/2022

Navigation pane

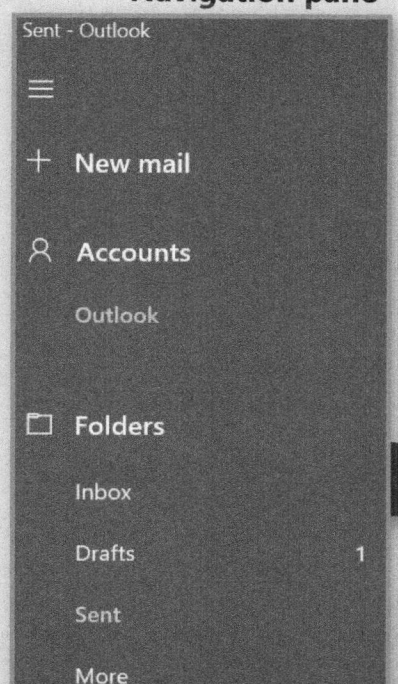

You will see a search bar, a refresh button, and a selection mode button in the messaging list pane.

You can use the search bar to look for specific terms or keywords in your emails. The refresh button will initiate a download and upload of all incoming and outgoing mails. The selection mode can select specific emails for deletion or move them into a different folder. Finally, the reading/writing pane is on the right side of the window.

HOW TO COMPOSE AN EMAIL

- Click the **+ New Mail button** in the navigation pane.

- A new writing pane will appear on the right of the window.

- Enter your recipient's email address in the 'To:' section.

  ◆ **You can send an email to multiple people simultaneously** by typing out each of their email addresses here. Your recipients will be able to see the other email addresses you have included.

  ◆ You can also CC people into your email. **CC stands for "carbon copy,"** and you can use this feature to send a copy of the email to somebody without them being the primary recipient. CC is a helpful feature when sending work emails: you can send something to a colleague and CC your manager to oversee all the communications.

- Enter a title for your email into the Subject line.

- Type out your email in the text field.

  ◆ You will see many features at the top of the writing pane, including **Format, Insert, Draw, and Options.**

    ◊ **FORMAT:** offers text formatting tools such as Bold, Italics, Underline, Bullet lists, and Styles.

◇ **INSERT:** allows you to attach files, tables, pictures, or links to your email.

◇ **DRAW:** You can input freehand notes or doodles into your email with Draw tools. You can also highlight or circle pieces of text.

◇ **THE OPTIONS TAB:** offers you spell checking tools, zoom and find tools, and the ability to flag your mail as high or low priority.

- When you have finished composing your email, click the **Send button.**

- You can use the **Delete button to discard anything in your email.**

Features Menu

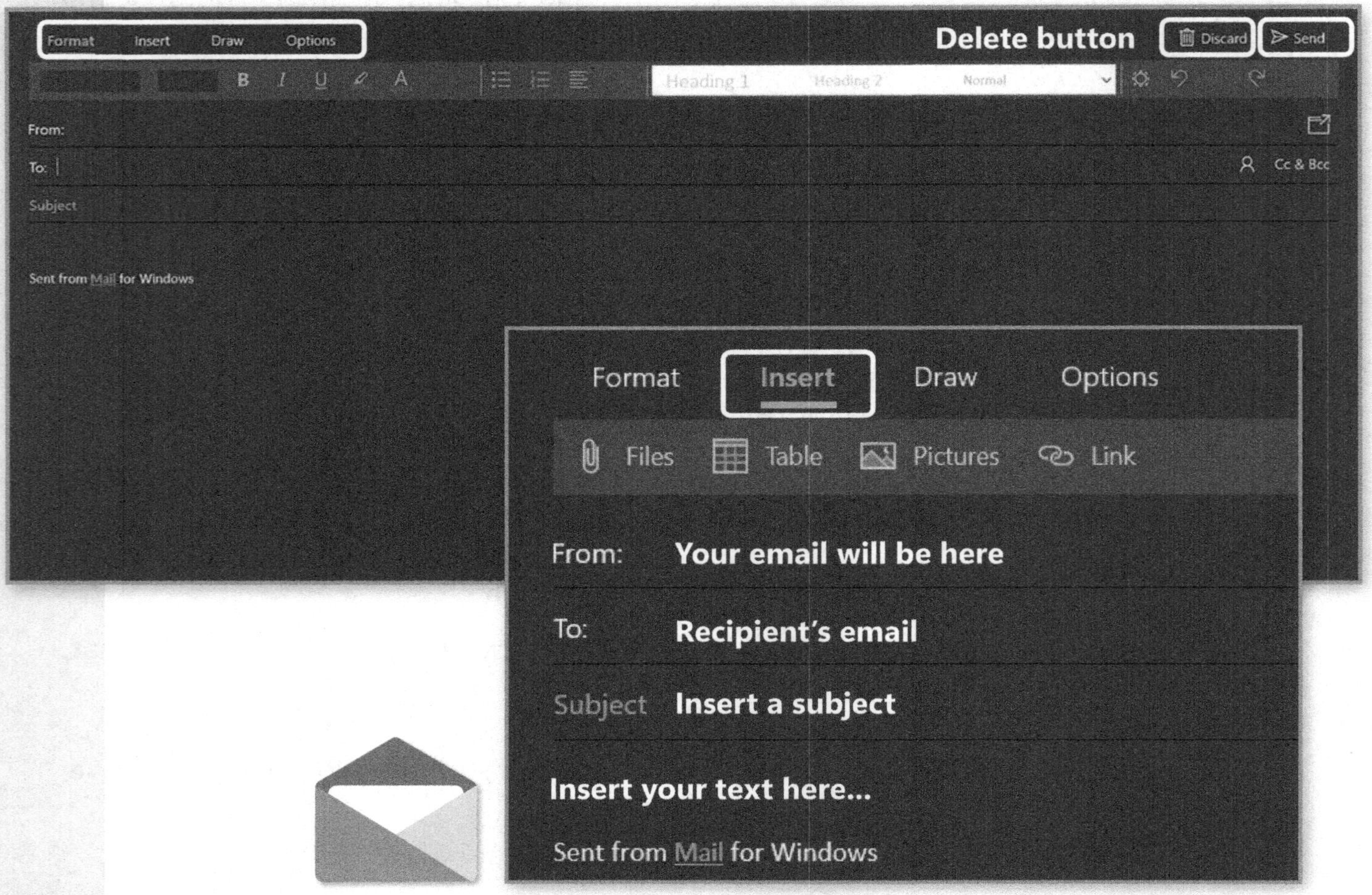

HOW TO READ AND REPLY TO EMAILS

- **To check for new mail, hit the refresh button at the top of your Mail app.**

- You will see a number next to your Inbox or other relevant folders if there are new mails to read. Click on the folder.

- Your messages will be shown in the messaging list pane, where **unread messages are highlighted with bold text** so that they are easier to find.

- Click on the unread email to view it in the reading pane on the right.

- To reply, click **'Reply'** at the top of the window.

- You can also choose **"Reply all"** to reply to everyone who received the original mail.

- **Forward** is used for sending a copy of the email and your response to a new email address.

- **You can archive your email:** this means that it will be removed from the Inbox but still stored in the Mail app so that you can access it.

- **You can also delete any emails you receive.**

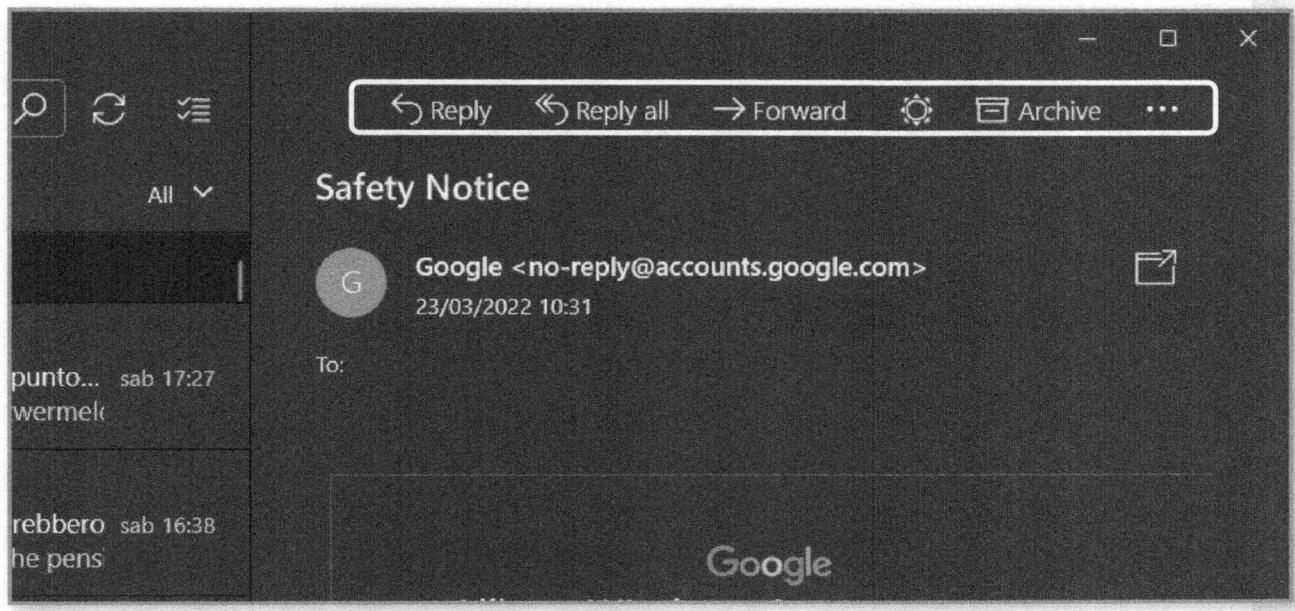

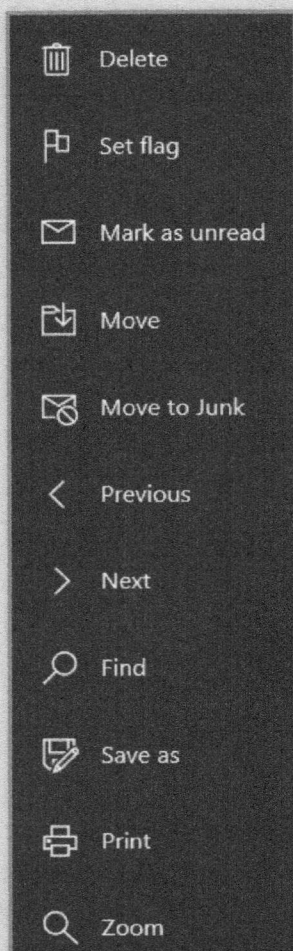

_ □ X

- There are a few other settings available in the **Tools button(...)** on the top right-hand side of the preview pane:

◊ **Set flag - assign a priority to the email.**
◊ **Mark as unread**
◊ **Move to a different folder.**
◊ **Move to the spam folder.**
◊ **View the previous mail or the next mail in your Inbox.**
◊ **Find a word or phrase in your email.**
◊ **Save as to store the mail in a text format.**
◊ **Print**
◊ **Zoom**

You can open any emails in a new window and view several windows simultaneously. To do this, double-click on the email in your inbox folder.

THE SPAM FOLDER

The spam folder is a valuable feature that helps you keep your Inbox clear of junk, clutter, advertisements, and other types of unwanted solicitation. The Mail app will automatically filter all your incoming emails for spam and place them into the spam folder. The Mail app looks for spoofed or unverifiable email addresses, blank messages, phishing scams, and mail similar to that you have previously marked as spam. The spam folder will be cleared out every 30 days.

If you receive spam in your Inbox, you can mark it as spam by clicking on the Tools icon in the top right of the window and selecting **'Mark as spam',** and this will help improve the filters used by the Mail app in the future.

CREATING FOLDERS AND ORGANIZING MAIL

Your mail will be sorted into different folders by default.
The primary folders include:

- **Inbox -** This is where all of your primary emails can be found.
- **Drafts -** this is where you can find emails that you have started writing but have not yet sent.

21°C
Sunny intervals

12:00 AM
01/01/2022

— ☐ ✕

- **Sent items** - this is where you find any emails sent by you.
- **Archive** - this is where you can find archived items.
- **Deleted Items** - the Mail app will store deleted emails for a limited time so that you can restore them if need be.
- **Junk Email** - This is where your junk and spam emails are stored for a limited time.

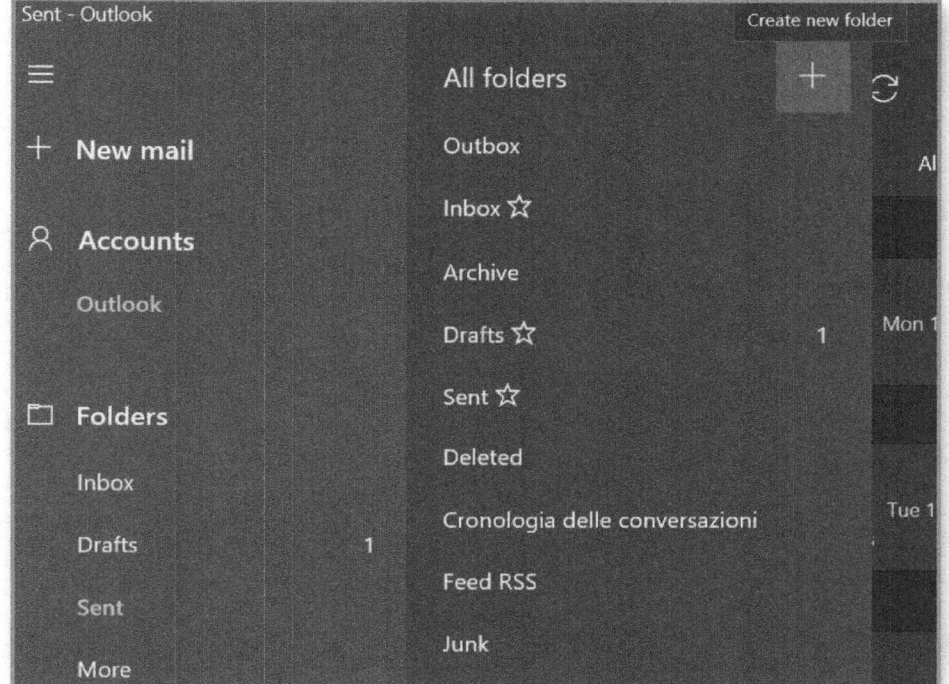

— ☐ ✕

You can sort and organize your emails by creating more personalized folders such as Work, Personal, Friends, Family, etc. **Right-click somewhere on the navigation pane to create a new folder and select "Create new folder."** You can also create subfolders by clicking on an existing folder and selecting "Create new subfolder." For example, you may have a Work folder with subfolders inside such as Boss, Colleagues, Clients, etc.

You can arrange and sort your folders in order of importance by dragging and dropping them into place. You can also mark specific folders as Favorites by right-clicking and selecting "Add to Favorites." Your Favorite folders are pinned near the top of the Folders section in the navigation pane, so they are always easy to access, and you do not have to scroll to look for them.

Folders offer many other useful tools. **Right-clicking on a folder allows you to rename, delete or move the folder to a new location.** You can empty a folder or mark all the emails inside as read. **You can also pin a folder to your Start menu, making it quick and easy to access your important emails.**

PERSONALIZING YOUR MAIL APP

You can control and change many of the Mail app's appearance and behaviors.

In **SETTINGS,** you can:

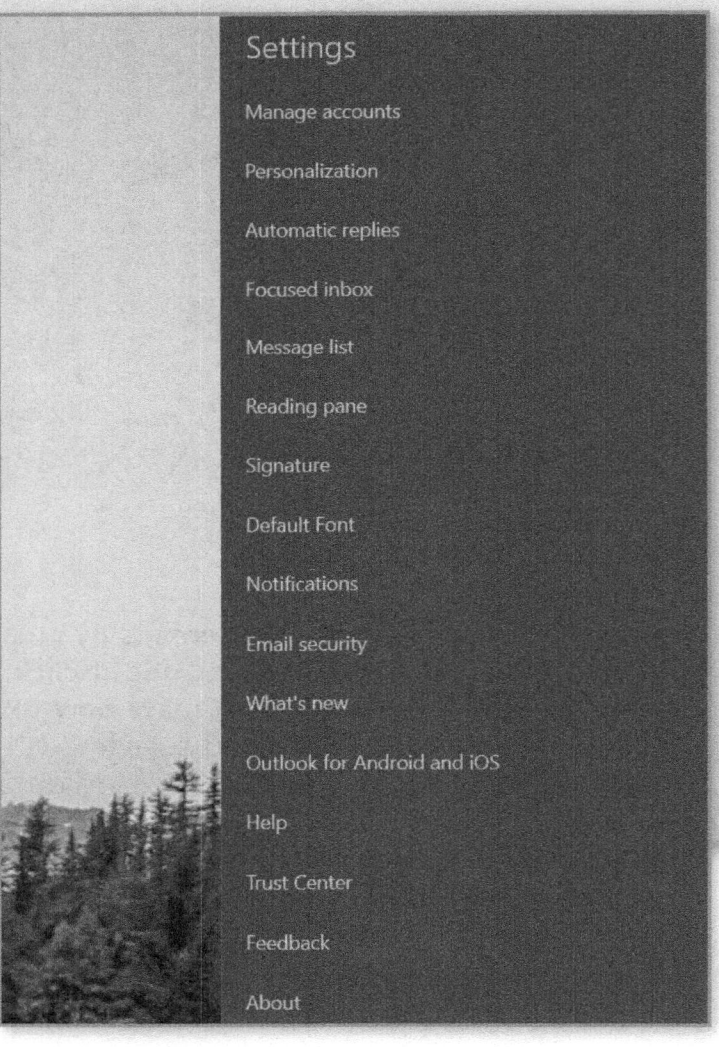

- **Personalize the messaging list pane** by changing swipe actions, organization, preview text, sender pictures, and image previews.

- **Personalize the reading pane** by changing auto-open, mark item as read, caret browsing, and external content settings.

- **Create a personalized email signature** to sign off on your emails.

- **Personalize your email notifications** with sounds, banners, and folders pinned to the Start menu.

- **Change the background image**, color folder, and message spacing, or switch to dark mode.

Settings

Manage accounts

Personalization

Automatic replies

Focused inbox

Message list

Reading pane

Signature

Default Font

Notifications

Email security

What's new

Outlook for Android and iOS

Help

Trust Center

Feedback

About

21°C
Sunny intervals

12:00 AM
01/01/2022

GOOGLE MAIL

Google Mail is an excellent alternative to the Mail app; however, it can only be used with 'Gmail' email addresses.

- To use Google mail, **visit www.gmail.com.**
- Enter your Gmail email address and password to log in.

The Gmail web page has a similar layout to the Windows 11 Mail app, showing a navigation pane on the left where you can access all of your folders. You can also access Google Meet, a video conferencing service, and Google Hangouts, a cross-platform messaging service.

Your emails are shown in the central part of the web page. Unread emails and folders containing unread emails will be highlighted in bold. Click on the emails to view the whole message.

You can quickly sort through your emails using the checkboxes on the right of each mail, selecting or deselecting to delete, mark as read, or move emails to a different folder.

COMPOSING AN EMAIL IN GOOGLE MAIL

To compose a new email, click the Compose button in the top left of the screen.

- A small window will pop up at the bottom right of the screen. Here you can input your recipient's email address, CC or BCC other contacts, and define the subject line.

- The toolbar at the bottom of this window offers several features:

  ◊ **Attach a file using File Explorer**
  ◊ **Insert a link**
  ◊ **Insert an emoji**
  ◊ **Insert a file using Google Drive**
  ◊ **Insert a photo**
  ◊ **Toggle confidential mode on or off**
  ◊ **Add a signature**

- To send a message, hit the Send button. By clicking the small arrow on the Send button, you can also choose to schedule a later time to send your message.

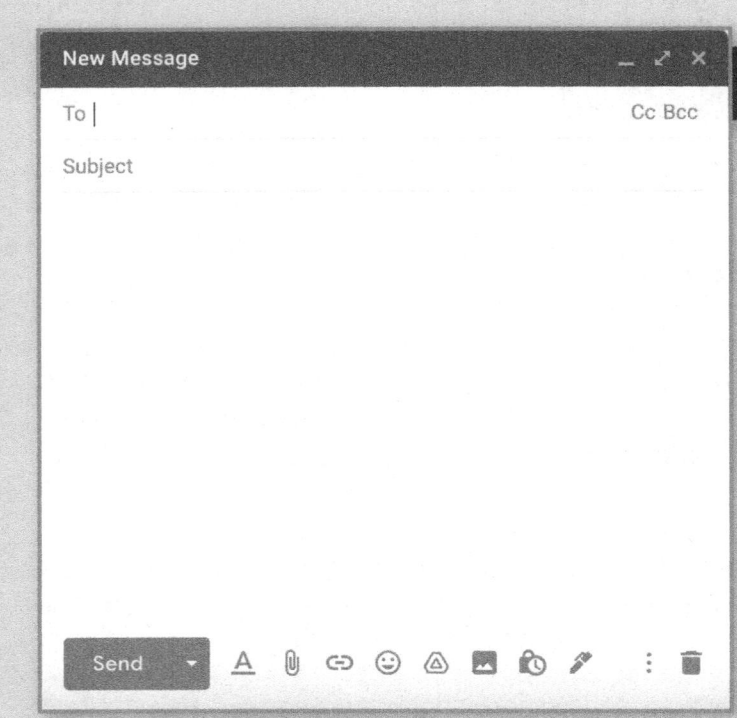

_ □ ✕

GOOGLE MAIL SETTINGS

The quick settings menu offers many options for personalizing the appearance of the web page including the layout, theme, inbox type and positioning of the reading pane.

You can access more settings by clicking the "See all settings" button at the top of the quick settings. This will direct you to a new web page and here you can access General, Labels, Inbox, Accounts and Import, Filters and Blocked addresses, Forwarding and POP/IMAP, Add-ons, Chat and Meet, Advanced, Offline and Theme settings.

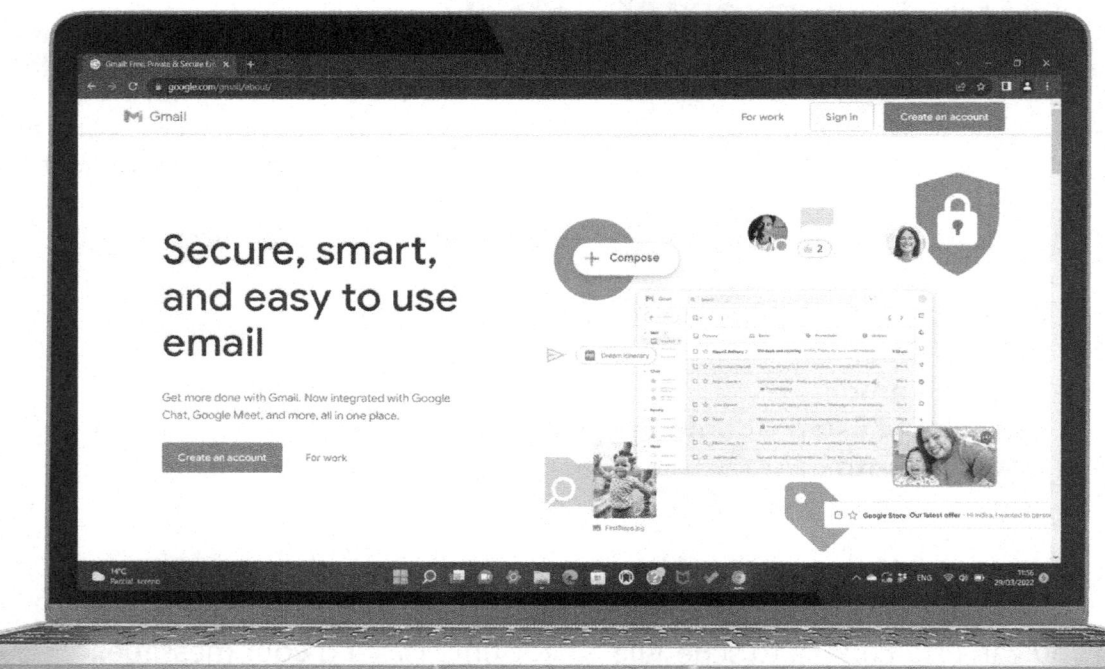

21°C
Sunny intervals

12:00 AM
01/01/2022

CHAPTER 7:

CONNECTING WITH MICROSOFT TEAMS

Teams is Microsoft's flagship video chat and instant messenger service, allowing you to set up one-on-one or group video calls and chat with your contacts. It offers many valuable features such as screen sharing, scheduling, messaging, and you can record your video chats. It is a great app to keep in touch with friends and family from anywhere in the world.

Teams has been separated into two apps: Chat and Teams. Both will come preinstalled with your operating system. The Chat app will only open as a small and simple pop-up window with a chat interface. To access the full features, you must open the Teams app. The default versions are intended for personal use only, and you may notice that some more advanced features are missing. To access these features, you will need to pay for the Business and School versions.

SETTING UP MICROSOFT TEAMS

You will find the icon for the Chat. You should see the app in your taskbar or search 'Chat' in the Start menu. However, if you cannot find Chat, you can download it from the Microsoft Store.

To make connecting more effortless, you can also download Microsoft Teams onto your Android or iOS device through the Google Play Store or the Apple App Store.

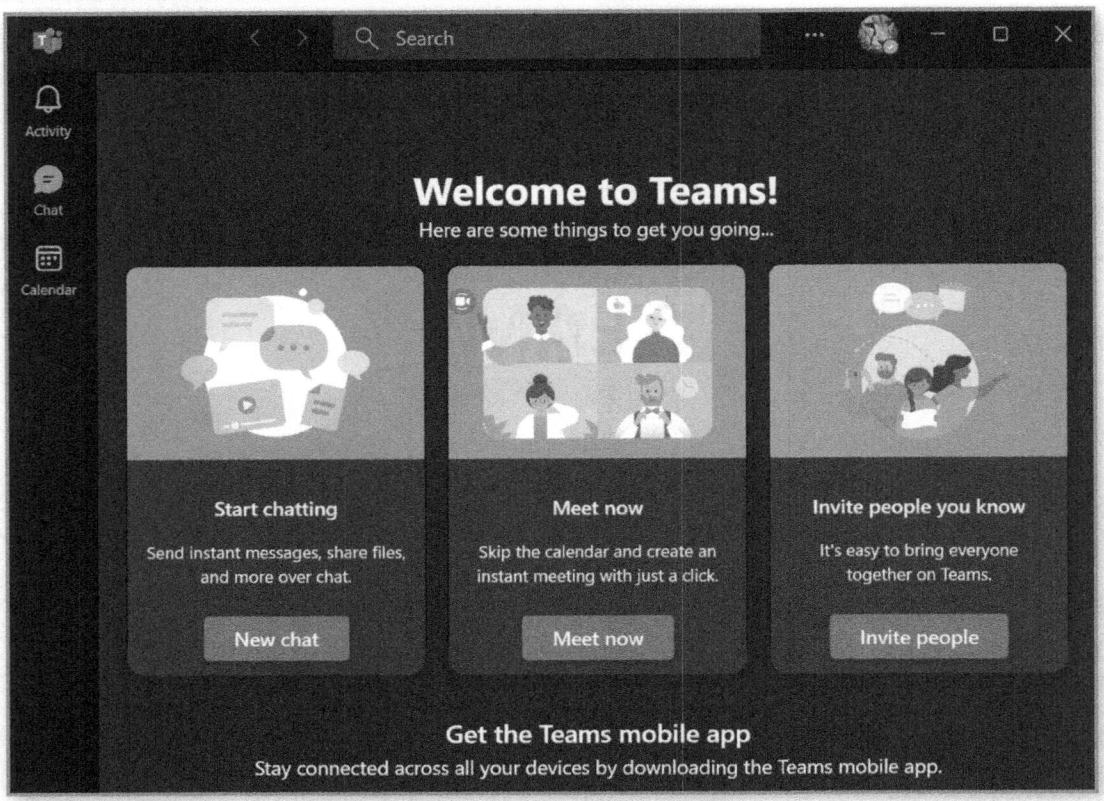

START-UP AND SIGN-IN

To open the Chat app, click on the icon in the taskbar or use the keyboard shortcut Ctrl+C.

- Upon your first time using the app, you will be asked to sign into an account. You should use your Microsoft account to sign into your Windows 11 device.

- Next, the Chat app will ask for your smartphone's phone number. Make sure to select the correct country code.

- A two-step verification code will be sent to this number. Confirm the code and then press next.

- The Chat app will begin syncing all of your contacts.

- To open the full version of Teams, type 'teams' into the Start menu and click the icon to launch the app.

21°C
Sunny intervals

12:00 AM
01/01/2022

START A NEW CONVERSATION

In Teams, click on the Chat icon found on the left side of the app window.

- Enter your contact's name, email, or phone number into the 'To:' section at the top of the screen.

- You can also start chatting with one of your groups.

- Start typing out your message at the bottom of the app window.

- You can easily add attachments to your messages or insert emojis, GIFs, and other types of fun graphics.

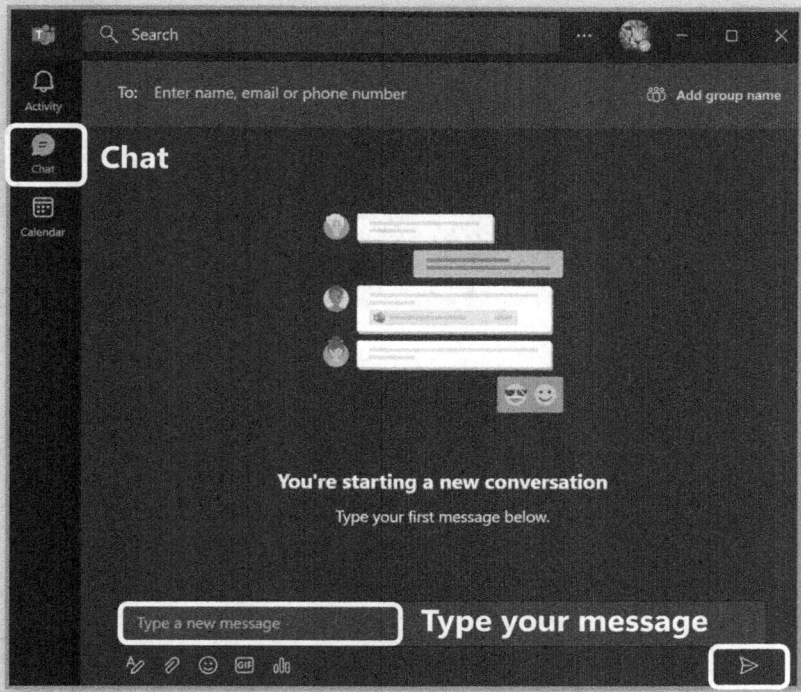

- Hit the small arrow icon on the bottom right to send your message.

START A VIDEO CHAT

To set up a video call, click on the Chat icon on the left side of the app.

- Select **"Start new meeting."**

- Give your meeting a name. This can be any identifying name so that your contacts will know what to expect when accepting your invitation.

- Click **"Get a link to share"** to generate a URL which you can then share with any of your contacts. They can access your meeting by using this link.

- You can also choose **"Start meeting,"** which will direct you to your video chat, where you can begin adding your contacts manually.

_ ☐ ✕

● Ensure your camera and microphone are correctly set up and ready to use before starting your meeting to avoid delays.

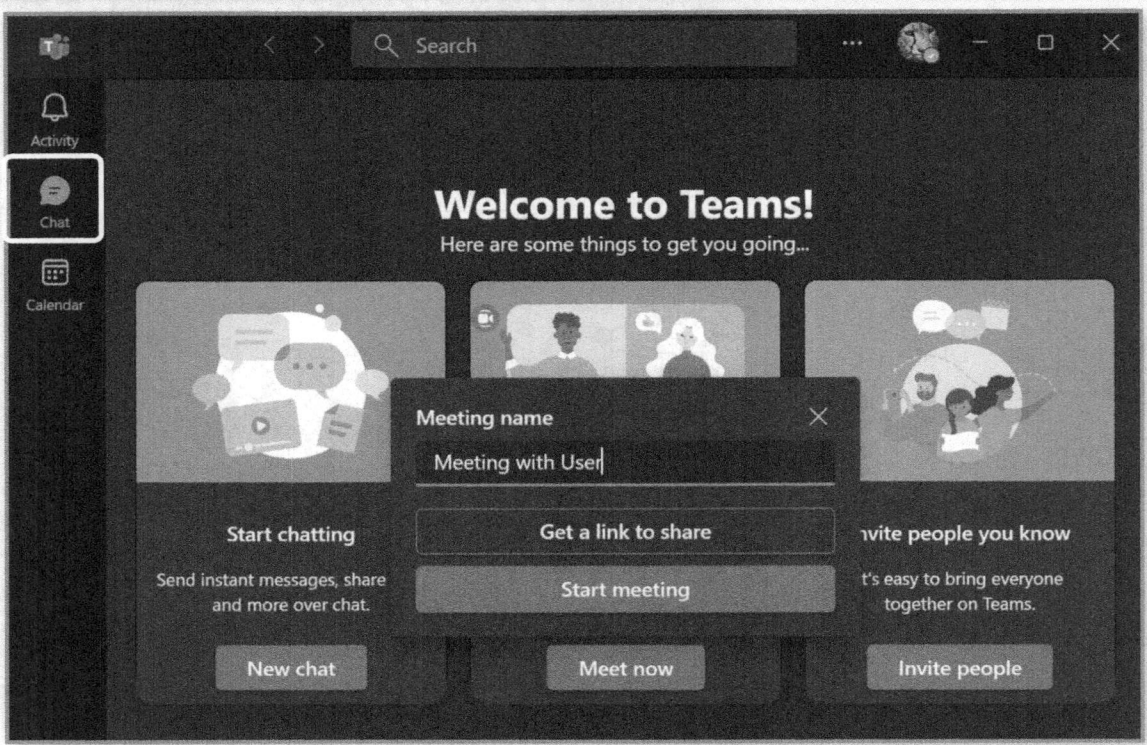

_ ☐ ✕

MANAGING A MEETING

Once in a meeting, you will see all participants displayed with each person in their own tile. The name of the meeting is shown at the top of the window in the title bar.
A toolbar runs across the top of the window with the following buttons:

1. **The duration of your meeting**

2. **The Teams icon** - click to see the names of all the participants in your meeting.

3. **The Chat icon -** click to open up a chat window with all the meeting's contacts.

4. **A "Raise your hand" icon** - click to let meetings' participants know you would like to speak. When another person presses this button, you will see a yellow box around their tile.

21°C
Sunny intervals

12:00 AM
01/01/2022

5. **The three-dots button** allows you to access additional settings:

   ◊ **Device settings**
   ◊ **Meeting options**
   ◊ **Meeting notes**
   ◊ **Meeting details**
   ◊ **Gallery/large gallery/together mode** - use these modes to change how you see the tiles of the participants in your meeting. You can view many small tiles, fewer larger tiles, only the active speaker, etc.
   ◊ **Fullscreen or Focus mode**.
   ◊ **Background effects** like plain colors, images from your File Explorer, or animated backgrounds.
   ◊ In the business version, you will also find the button to record your meetings here.

6. **A button to turn your camera on or off.**

7. **A button to turn your microphone on or off.**

8. **A screen sharing button** so that others can see what is on your screen.

9. **The Leave button** to end or leave an ongoing meeting.

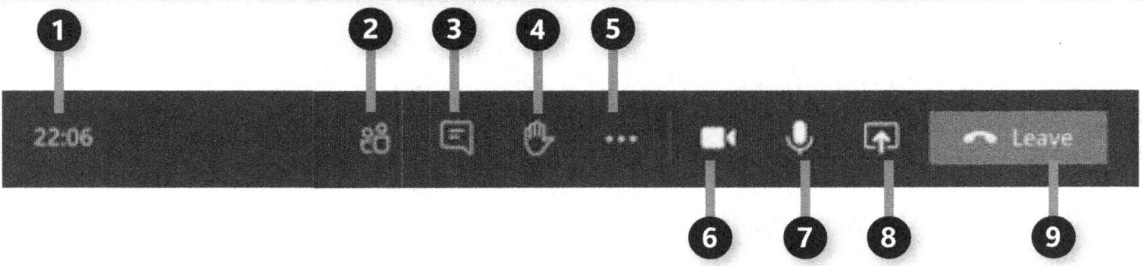

INVITE CONTACTS

Add your contacts to the Teams app so that you can quickly initiate conversations or meetings with them simply by typing as name rather than going and finding their email address or phone number.

- **Click the Chat icon** in the left side of the app and then **select "Invite people."**

_ □ ✕

- You can add your contacts by typing out their name, email address, phone number, and any other information you may need.

CREATE A GROUP

Use groups to connect with different categories of your contacts easily. For example, you can create groups for your grandchildren, one side of your family, colleagues working on a specific project with you, and more.

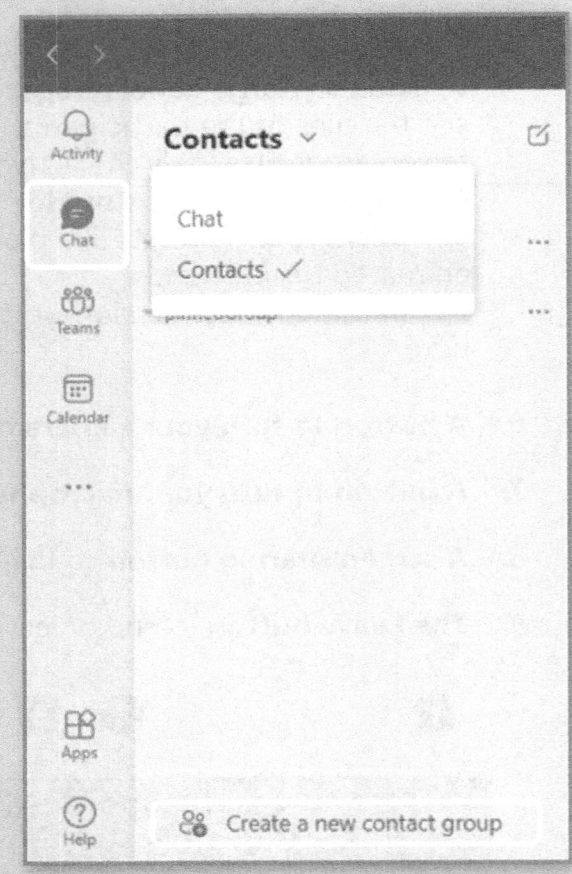

- **To create a group, click on the Chat icon** on the left side of the app.

- **Select 'Contacts'** from the drop-down menu at the top of the screen.

- Then select the **"Create a new contact group"** at the bottom.

- Add in all the contacts you wish and give your group a name.

- Now, you can begin conversations or video chats with the group rather than adding individual contacts.

- **You can add up to 64 contacts in a group.**

USING THE CALENDAR APP WITH TEAMS

Schedule meetings ahead of time using the integrated Calendar app.

- **Click on Calendar** on the left side of the Teams app.

- **Click on the day and select a time** to schedule your meeting.

- Then **right-click on the calendar**, or click the purple "+ New meeting" button.

21°C
Sunny intervals

12:00 AM
01/01/2022

_ □ ✕

- **Give your meeting a name, and invite all the contacts** you would like to join in the video chat.

- Make sure to double-check that the date and time are correct before saving.

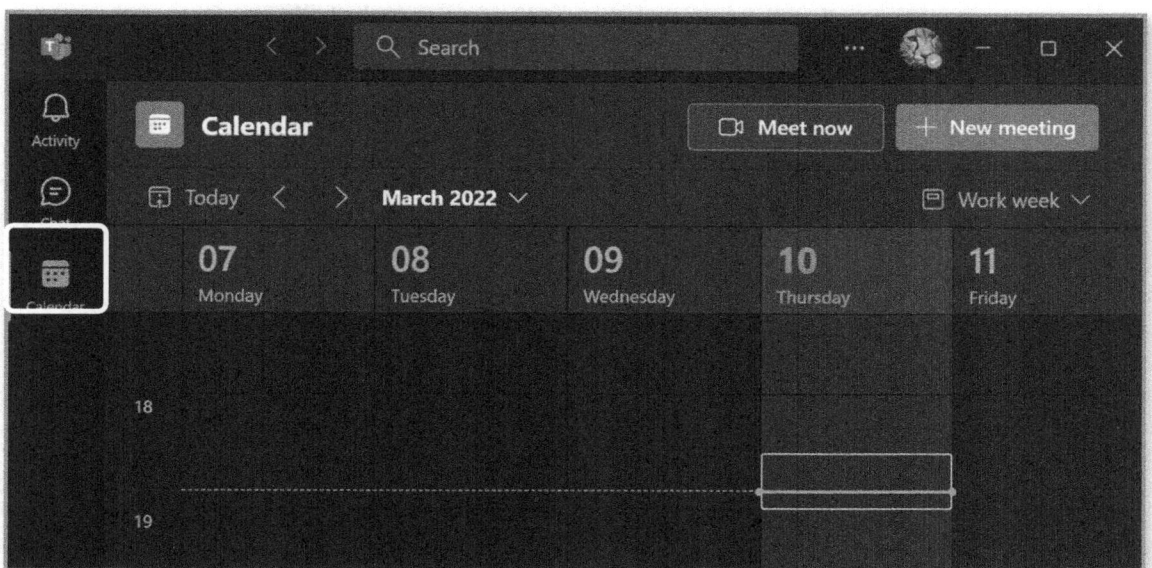

_ □ ✕

SETTINGS

Access settings for the Team app by clicking the three-dots icon on the top right side of the window, which you can find next to your profile picture.
You will see a settings window with:

- **General -** Change your language, time, date format settings; and allow Teams to start automatically upon start-up.

- **Notifications -** Set your notification sounds for incoming messages or video chat requests; mute alerts; customize your notifications by setting alerts for specific contacts or activities; and change how you see notifications on your screen.

- **Appearance and accessibility -** Select between Light, Dark, and High contrast themes, and turn animations on or off.

_ ☐ ✕

- **People -** Manage your contacts and change the permissions for different people.

- **Privacy -** Change Teams privacy settings to public or private, allowing people to see your activity or requiring them to have a link before they can join a chat or video call.

- **Plans and upgrades -** access Business or School versions of Teams by upgrading your subscription plan and entering your monthly or yearly billing payment details.

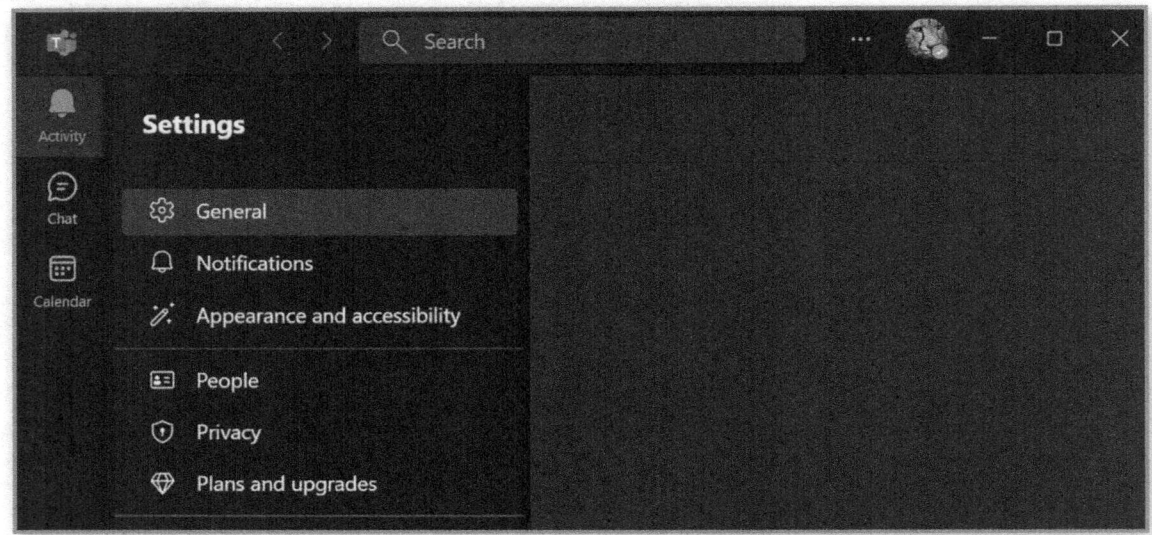

_ ☐ ✕

THE CHAT APP

Open the simplified and reduced version of Teams by clicking the Chat icon in your taskbar. This will open a small pop-up window where you can see your recent chats and synced contacts.

- Click the **'Meet' button** at the top of the window to begin a new meeting.

- Click the **'Chat' button** at the top of the window to begin a new chat.

- You can click the **"Open Microsoft Teams" button** at the bottom of this window to open the full version of the Teams app.

21°C
Sunny intervals

12:00 AM
01/01/2022

CHAPTER 8:

APPS FOR YOUR DAILY ROUTINE

— ☐ ✕

Windows 11 offers a wide range of tools that you can use to improve your productivity and make your daily routine easier and more efficient. You can find these apps in the Microsoft Store.

🔍 MICROSOFT APPS

MICROSOFT TO DO

Microsoft To Do is a task management app that works as a to-do list, helping you to keep track of all the tasks you need to complete and allowing you to mark them off when completed. You can sync the To Do app with your smartphone so that you can access your lists when you are out and about.

The To Do app comes standard in Windows 11.

- **Open To Do by clicking typing 'TO DO' in the ▣ Start menu .**

- Sign in with your Microsoft account the first time you use the app.

  ◊ Click **'Yes'** to pin the ap to the taskbar for easy access.

- The app will open showing a navigation pane on the left and a focus pane on the right.

- In the navigation pane you will see your account, a search bar, My Day, Important,

Planned, Assigned to me, Tasks, Getting started, and lists like Groceries:

- ◊ **My Day -** all tasks due today.
- ◊ **Important -** tasks marked as important.
- ◊ **Planned -** tasks with upcoming due dates.
- ◊ **Assigned -** tasks assigned to you using the Planner app.
- ◊ **Tasks -** Uncategorized tasks.
- ◊ **Groceries -** A type of smart list.

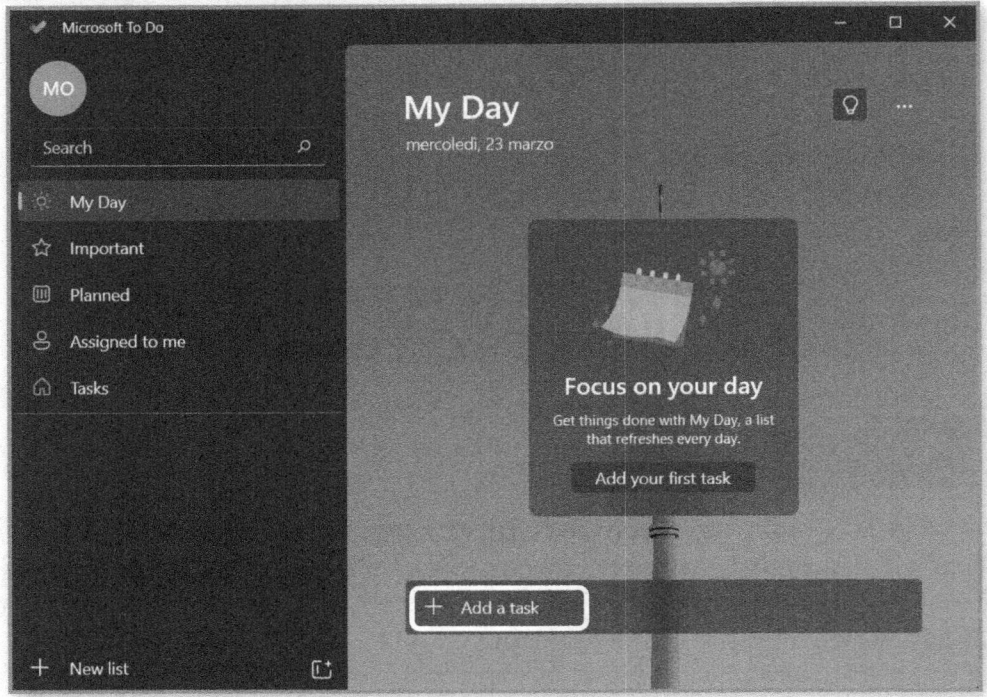

CREATING A TASK

Click on Tasks, or select one of the categories, lists, or groups.

- Click **"Add a task"** at the bottom of the task tab and write your task.

- Use the icons to the right to set a due date, a reminder, or a repeat event.

- **Press Enter to save the task**.

21°C
Sunny intervals

12:00 AM
01/01/2022

- You can modify your tasks once they have been added by clicking on them.

- Move tasks into a different list or group by clicking and dragging them into place. You can also right-click on a task and choose "Move task to..." to select a new list.

- Right-click on a task to add it to the **"My Day" list.** This action will set the task's due date to the current day.

- Mark a task as important by right-clicking and selecting "Mark as important."

SUBTASKS

You can add subtasks when a task has many steps to remember. For example, if you set a task to Get craft supplies, you can add a step for each of the supplies you need.

- Click **"Add Steps,"** write out the step, and hit Enter to continue adding steps.

ADD AN ATTACHMENT

You can attach any file to your tasks, including pictures, documents, spreadsheets, or scans.
- Click on your Task and select **"Add file"** to open File Explorer.

- Select the file you want to attach and hit Enter.

ADD NOTES

More detailed notes can also be added to each task allowing you to elaborate on what needs to get done.

- Click on your Task and select **"Add note"** to write a short description.

DELETE TASKS

Select it and then click the rubbish bin in the bottom right corner to delete a task.

_ □ ✕

COMPLETING TASKS

To mark a task as complete, click on the circle to the left of the task's name.

- Completed tasks will be struck through and moved to the bottom of the task pane in a new list called **'Completed.'**

- The Completed list is not shown in the navigation pane, but you can enable this feature:

- Click on your account at the top of the navigation pane select: **SETTINGS > SMART LIST > COMPLETED.** Click the toggle to enable Completed lists in the navigation pane.

- You can uncheck the circle to mark a task as incomplete.

CREATE A LIST

You can create several lists to keep all of your tasks organized. Lists will be shown in the navigation pane.

- Create a new list by **clicking "New list"** at the bottom of the navigation pane.

- Select a name for your list and hit Enter.

- Begin adding tasks to the list by clicking **"Add a task"** in the task pane.

CREATE A GROUP

Create groups to organize all of your lists.

- **To create a new group, click the "Create a new group" icon** at the bottom right of the navigation pane.

- You can **create new lists** to go inside this group by **right-clicking and selecting "New list."**

21°C
Sunny intervals

12:00 AM
01/01/2022

_ □ ✕

ORGANIZING TASKS, LISTS, AND GROUPS

You can sort the tasks in each list by clicking the tools icon (three dots) in the top right of the task pane. Tasks can be sorted by Importance, Due Date, Added to My Day, Alphabetically, or by Creation Date.

LIST TOOLS

Right-click on a list in the navigation pane to bring up options such as Rename list, Share List, Move list to, Print list, Email list, Pin to Start, Duplicate list, or Delete list.

Change the list-icon to an emoji or symbol by right-clicking on the list, selecting 'Rename,' then clicking on the icon. This will bring up a selection of emojis from which to choose.

SHORTCUTS FOR TO DO

- **Add a task - Ctrl+N**
- **Create a new list - Ctrl+L**
- **Add a task to My Day - Ctrl+T**
- **Complete a task - Ctrl+D**
- **Search - Ctrl+F**
- **Sync - Ctrl+R**
- **Print - Ctrl+P**

🔍 **CALENDAR APP**

The Calendar app comes standard with Windows 11. You can see it at a glance by clicking the time and date icon on the right of your taskbar. To see all the Calendar features, open it by clicking the Calendar app icon in the Start menu or on your taskbar.

The Calendar app is linked with the Mail, People, and To Do apps, allowing you to switch between and share data from each app. You will find icons for each of these apps at the bottom of the navigation pane.

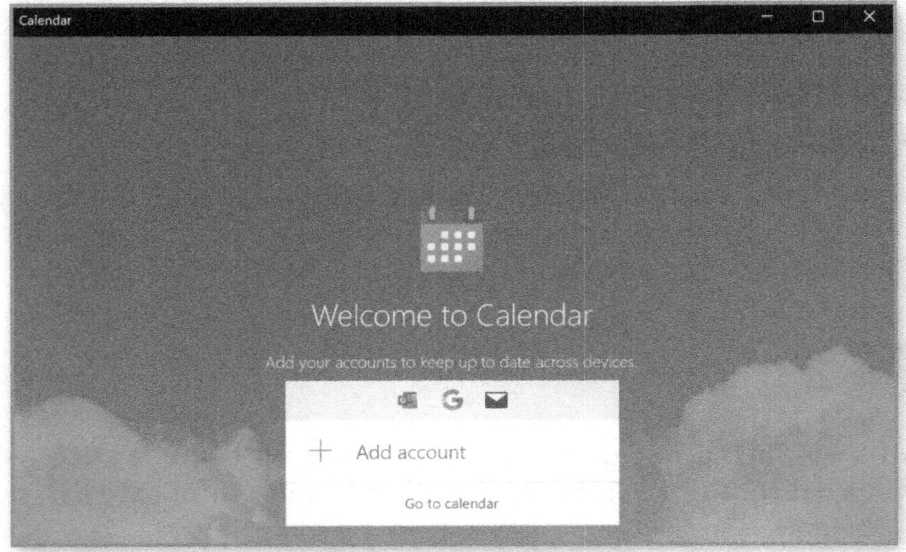

_ ▢ ✕

ADD AN ACCOUNT

The Calendar app must link with an email account such as your Microsoft or Google account.

- To add an account, click **SETTINGS > MANAGE ACCOUNTS > ADD ACCOUNT.** Input your email address and password. Allow any permissions, and your account info will sync with the Calendar app.

- You can add multiple accounts using these steps.

MANAGING CALENDARS

You can add many calendars using the app, including Holidays, Birthdays, Contacts, and custom calendars.

- **To add a new calendar, click "Add calendars" at the bottom of the navigation pane.** Choose what type of calendar you would like to add.

- You can show or hide calendars to reduce clutter by checking or unchecking the boxes to the left of the calendar's name.

- Calendars can be removed by right-clicking and selecting **"Remove calendar."**

21°C
Sunny intervals

12:00 AM
01/01/2022

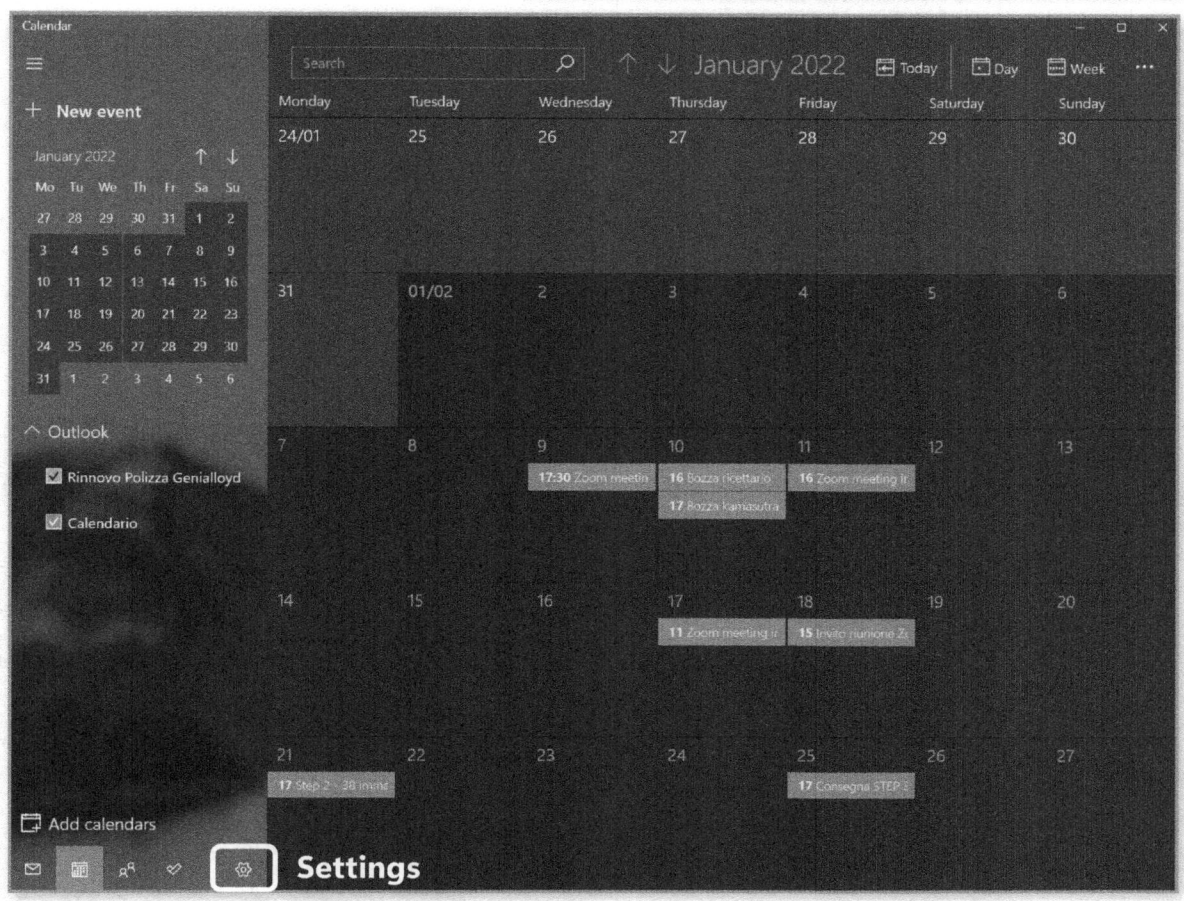

CREATE AN EVENT

There are several types of events you can create in the Calendar app:

1. QUICK EVENT

To create a Quick Event, open the Calendar app and click on the day you want to schedule the event.

- A small pop-up will appear where you can input the event name, time, location, and reminder information.

- Events are set to **"Add day"** by default. You can uncheck this box and set start and end times.

— ▢ ✕

- You can also set an icon or emoji by clicking the gray circle to the left of the event name.

- To change which account or calendar the event will be linked with, click the title bar at the top of this pop-up and select the account from the drop-down menu.

Click 'Save' to add this event to your calendar.

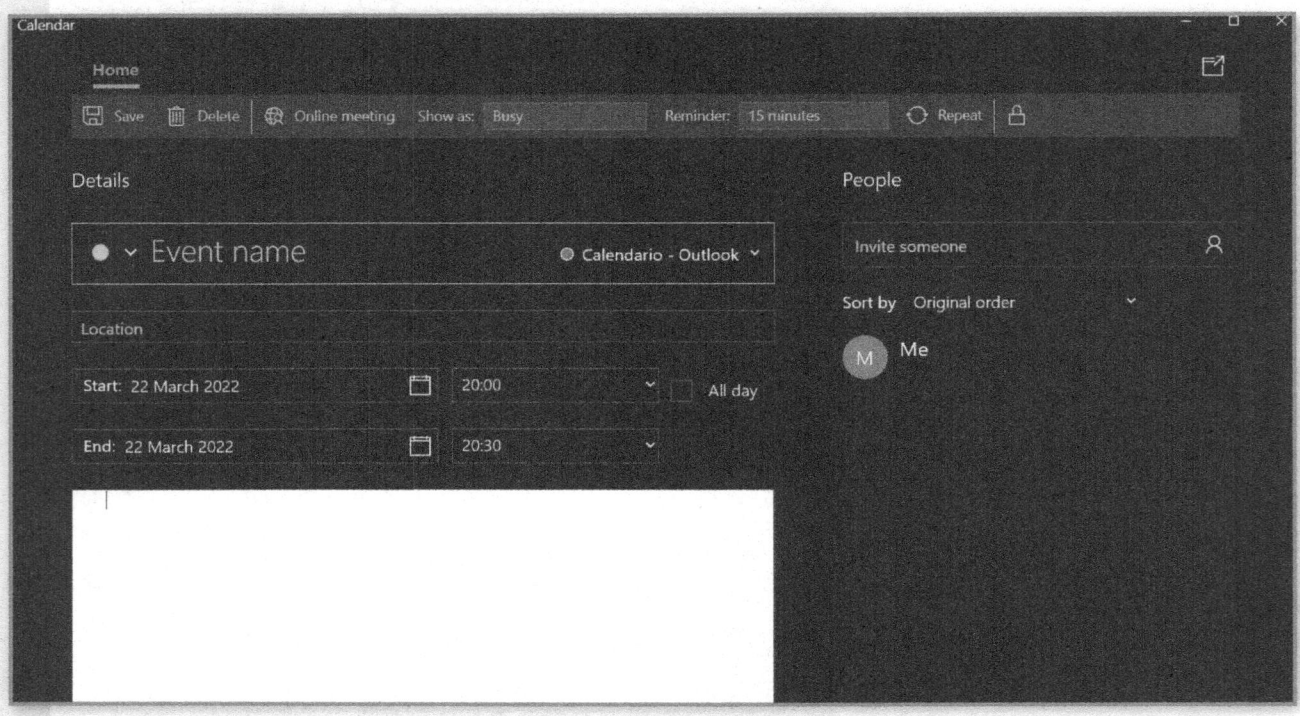

— ▢ ✕

2. DETAILED
EVENT

To add a Detailed Event, click "New event" at the top of the navigation pane, or select "More details" at the bottom of the Quick Event pop-up.

- A new pane will open where you can input the name of your detailed event, select an icon, and choose which calendar to save it to.

- Set the event location. The app will find matching places, which you can use to get directions.

21°C
Sunny intervals

12:00 AM
01/01/2022

- Add notes using the text box at the bottom of this page.

- Options to save, delete, schedule an online meeting, set status, set a reminder, or repeat the event are in the toolbar at the top.

- You can invite people to join your event using the contact list on the right.

- Click the 'Save' button to add the event to the calendar.

3. GROUP EVENT

You can create a group event by adding contacts to a detailed event. The contacts will receive a notification for the event, and it will be added to their calendars.

Click 'Send' instead of 'Save;' this will send out invitations to each of your contacts for them to accept or decline.

4. REPEATING EVENT

**You can create repeating events **This is for birthdays, anniversaries, weekly workouts, or other events that repeat each year or week.

- Configure the repeat cycle by selecting daily, weekly, monthly, or yearly repetitions. You can choose to repeat the event every day, every second day, every three days, etc. You can set a few other options here to configure the repeat event precisely as you need it.

- Make sure to set an end date, or the event will repeat indefinitely into the future.

- **Click 'Save' to store the event in your calendar.**

5. SHARING A CALENDAR

You can share calendars with your contacts, allowing them to view or edit the events.

- Right-click on the calendar you want to share in the navigation pane and select **"Share calendar."**

_ □ ✕

- Enter the email address or addresses of your contacts, then hit enter.

- You will see a drop-down menu to choose if that contact can edit or only view the event.

- **Click 'Share' to finish.**

🔍 SEARCH AND EXPLORE WITH MAPS APP

The Maps app allows you to search, explore and navigate your world. You can use it to get driving, walking, or transit directions, check traffic and congestion, mark your parked location, find information and reviews about businesses, and explore the world in 3D or through 360° panoramas using Streetside views.

USING MAPS

The Maps app will show a map that displays your current location as long as you are connected to the internet.

- Click on the map and drag it around to view different areas.

- The sidebar on the right of the map contains different tools such as map orientation, imagery, map views, and zoom in or out.

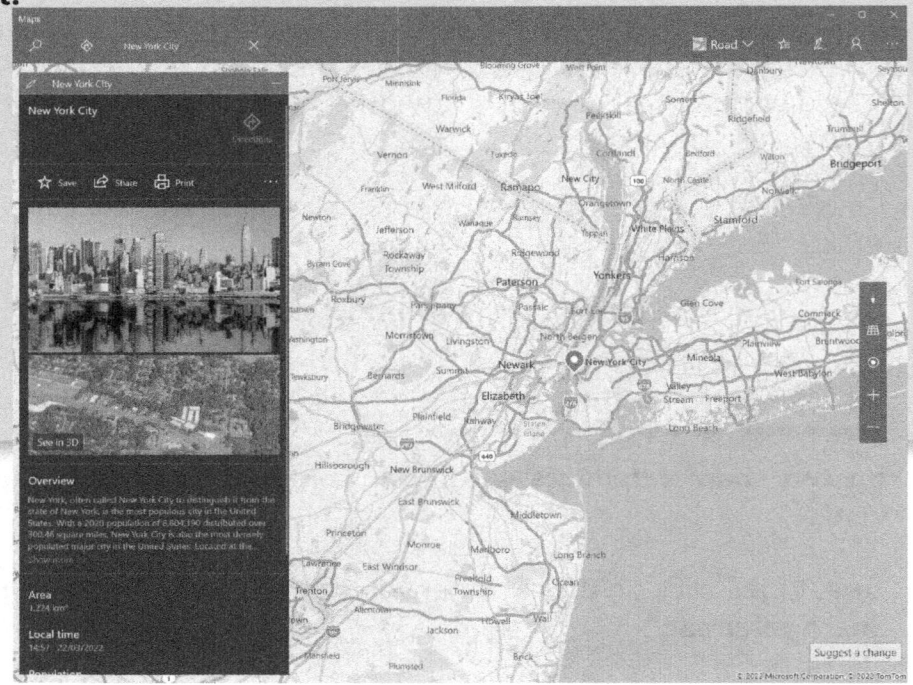

21°C
Sunny intervals

12:00 AM
01/01/2022

_   □   ✕

SEARCH

You can search for different locations using the Map app by typing a keyword or address into the search bar on the top left of the window.
The search results will provide you with the name of the location, its street address, and an overview.

NAVIGATION

You can click on the 'Directions' button to get turn-by-turn directions from your current location, as well as traffic information to make your commute quick and easy.
Maps also show you attractions like restaurants, shops, hotels, or banks near the location you are searching for, making it easy to plan trips.

FAVORITES

You can save various locations as favorites. These will be stored in the Maps app so that you can find them in the future.

- To add a favorite location, you will have to search for it.

- Select the correct result and click on the star icon found under the location's name.

- Add a nickname for your favorite locations.

- You can find your favorites at the top of the window, next to the Search and Direction icons.

STREET VIEW

To see a 360° view of a street, click on the Map views button found in the sidebar on the right side of the map.

- Turn on the Streetside feature.

_ □ ✕

- Now you can select any location on the map highlighted in blue.

- You can also search for a specific location using the search feature and click on the Streetside icon.

- This will place you in Street View mode. You can move around on the street by dragging in any direction or clicking the arrows shown on the screen.

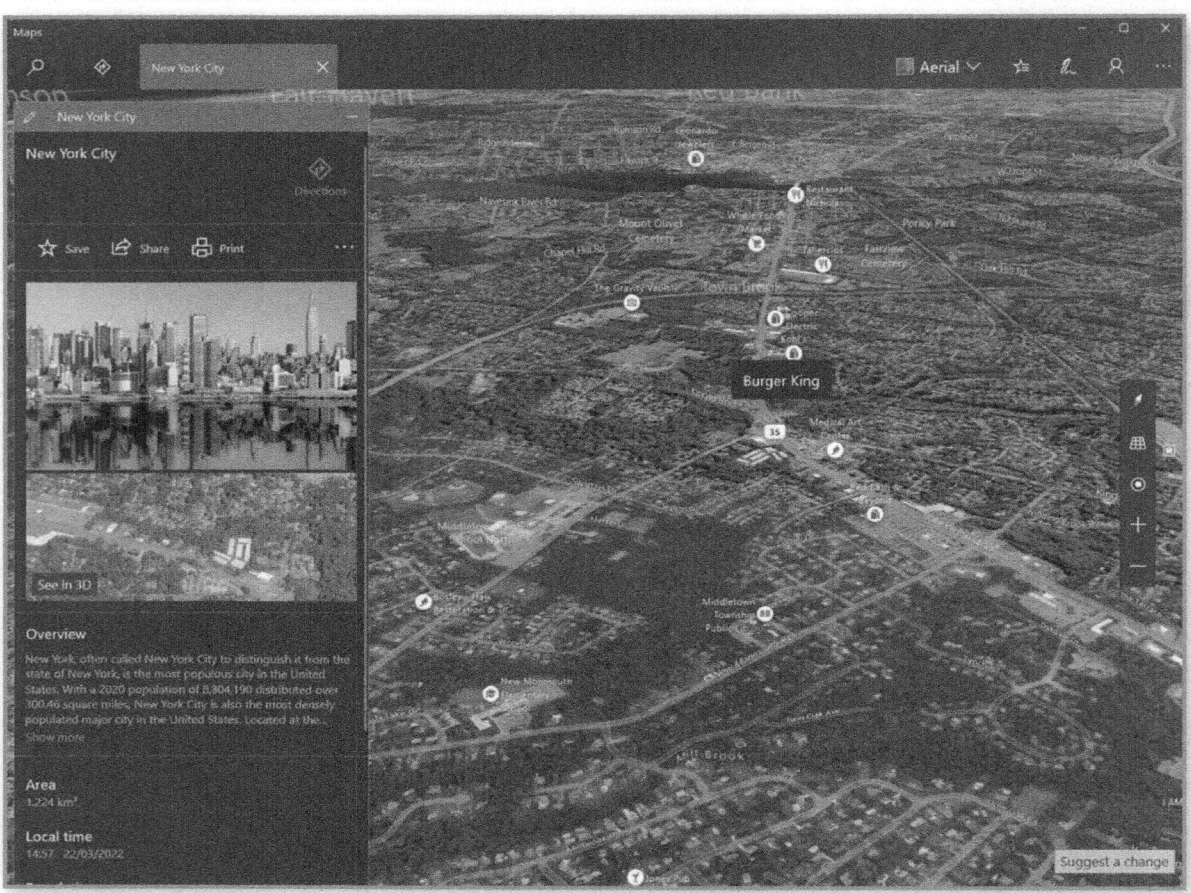

_ ☐ ✕

🔍 WRITE A DOCUMENT WITH WORDPAD

WordPad is a simple text-editing program that you can use to view, edit and create documents. It comes standard with Windows 11 and is a good alternative to the more expensive, subscription-based Microsoft Word. WordPad is not as advanced as Microsoft Word, and you may miss some features.

- **Open WordPad by clicking the ▪▪ Start menu and searching 'WordPad.'** Click on the app icon to begin running the program.

- A window will open, showing a toolbar running across the top part of the screen and a blank page taking up the rest of the space.

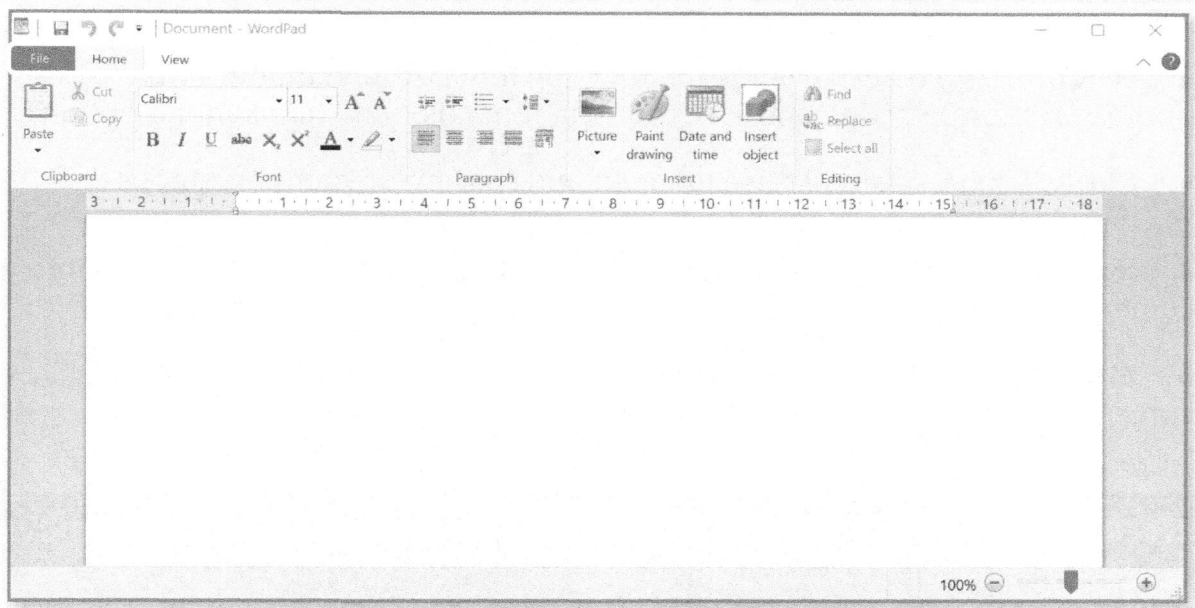

_ ☐ ✕

USING WORDPAD

Click on the blank page to begin writing.
The toolbar contains a File tab, Home tab, and View tab:

_ ◻ ✕

- Click on the **FILE TAB** to access settings such as: open a new document, open a document from File Explorer, save your document, save your document in a specific location or file format, print, page setup, send in an email, or to exit the program.

- Click on the **HOME TAB** to view the document and the toolbar with various features.

- Click on the **VIEW TAB** to zoom in or out, show or hide the ruler and status bar, and change word wrapping and measurement settings.

FORMATTING TOOLS

WordPad offers a good variety of formatting tools to create and customize documents. You will see these tools organized into different sections:

- **CLIPBOARD -** these tools are for cutting, copying, and pasting pieces of text or images.

- **FONT** - here, you can change the font, the font size, and other formatting options like bold, italics, superscript, and subscript and font color and highlighting options.

- **PARAGRAPH -** change the alignment and spacing of your paragraphs.

- **INSERT -** insert pictures, Paint drawings, date and time, or other objects into your document.

- **EDITING -** find, replace or select different words, phrases, or sections in your document.

CONVERTING WORDPAD DOCS INTO MICROSOFT WORD DOCS - GOOGLE DRIVE

WordPad offers a limited number of file formats to save your document. This includes Rich Text, Open XML, OpenDocument, or plain text. Unfortunately, WordPad does not allow you to save your files as Word documents, which are the most widely used format. However, there are ways around this.

- **You can save your document in a Rich Text Format and upload it into your Google Drive.**

21°C
Sunny intervals

12:00 AM
01/01/2022

— ☐ ✕

- **You can get Google Drive by setting up a free Google email address and visiting drive.google.com.** This is an online storage space to save documents, pictures, and other files. It comes standard with 15GB of space, but you can also purchase more if you run out.

- **Drag your Rich Text format document into your google drive** and then click on it to open the document in Google Docs.

- From the toolbar at the top of the page, select **FILE > DOWNLOAD > MICROSOFT WORD.**

- This will save a copy of your WordPad document as a Microsoft Word document in your Downloads library.

- The Microsoft Word document can be more easily shared with your contacts.

🔍 STICKY NOTES

The Sticky Notes app allows you to create digital post-it notes that you can stick to your Desktop. You can use them to keep small notes, motivational quotes, reminders, or to-do lists.

- **Open the Sticky Notes app by searching "sticky notes" in the ▪ Start menu.**

- A window will open, and you will see a straightforward app with few buttons.

- The settings menu offers sign-in, general settings, and color settings, allowing you to switch from light to dark mode.

- You should sign into your Microsoft account so that you can safely save your sticky notes.

CREATE A NEW STICKY NOTE

Click on the + icon in the top right of the window.

- A yellow sticky note will appear on the side of the app window.

- Type your note in this space and use the simple formatting tools to edit it or insert a picture.

- You will see that a summary of your sticky note appears in the app's main window.

- **Click on the Settings icon (three dots) on the yellow sticky note to change its color or delete it.**

- Sticky notes that you have created will remain open even when you close the app window.

- You can create and display many sticky notes simultaneously, and you can change their colors and sizes to differentiate between them.

🔍 USING CORTANA

Cortana is a virtual assistant that responds to voice commands. It can help you interact with your computers, programs, and apps.

- **Open the app by typing 'Cortana' into the ▪▪ Start menu.**

- Sign in using your Microsoft account.

- **Click "Accept and continue"** to grant Cortana access to some of your personal information.

- Cortana is now ready to use. In the app's window, you can type out a request and press Enter or click the microphone button and speak into your device's microphone to ask Cortana a question.

Cortana can provide basic technical support and work with the Control Panel or File Explorer so that you can easily access a setting or file. You can use Cortana to fetch news or weather information, and it can also provide results from a web search.

21°C
Sunny intervals

12:00 AM
01/01/2022

CHAPTER 9:

TAKING PHOTOS
AND MORE

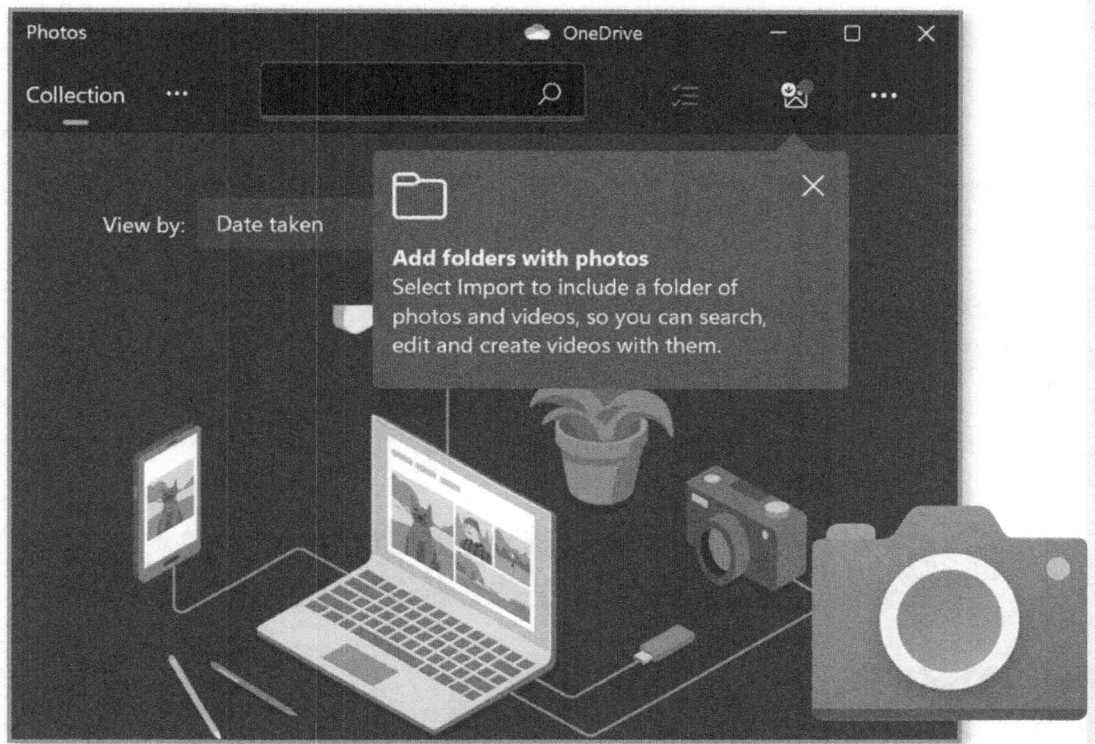

🔍 TAKING PHOTOS AND VIDEOS

With Windows 11, you can easily take photos or videos and edit your media using some of Microsoft's default programs. If you are using a Windows 11 laptop or mobile device like a tablet, it will likely come with a built-in camera that you can use to take pictures or videos.

_ □ ✕

- **Find out if you have a camera by typing 'Camera' into the** 🔲 **Start menu.**

- If you see an icon appear, click on it to **open the** 📷 **Camera app.**

- To use your camera, make sure it points towards the subject you want to capture in a photo or video. Check your screen to see a preview of the image and ensure everything is centered and framed correctly.

- **When you are ready, click the 'Capture' button** on the left of the bottom of the screen.

- **First, click on the Video icon in the Camera app to take a video.**

- **Press the 'Record' button to begin capturing footage**, and then press the same button to stop recording when you are finished.

VIEWING YOUR PHOTOS AND VIDEOS

Windows 11 will save all the content you capture using your built-in camera to the "Camera Roll" folder in your Pictures Library. You can access this media using File Explorer.

🔍 USING THE PHOTOS APP

IMPORT PICTURES FROM YOUR CAMERA

You can import images and videos from a camera, smartphone, or tablet onto your Windows 11 computers so that you can store, view, and edit them.

- Begin by plugging your camera, smartphone, or tablet into your computer using the USB cable, which should be provided with your device.

- You should be able to see a small USB icon in your system tray on the right side of your taskbar if you have done this correctly.

21°C
Sunny intervals

◁))

12:00 AM
01/01/2022

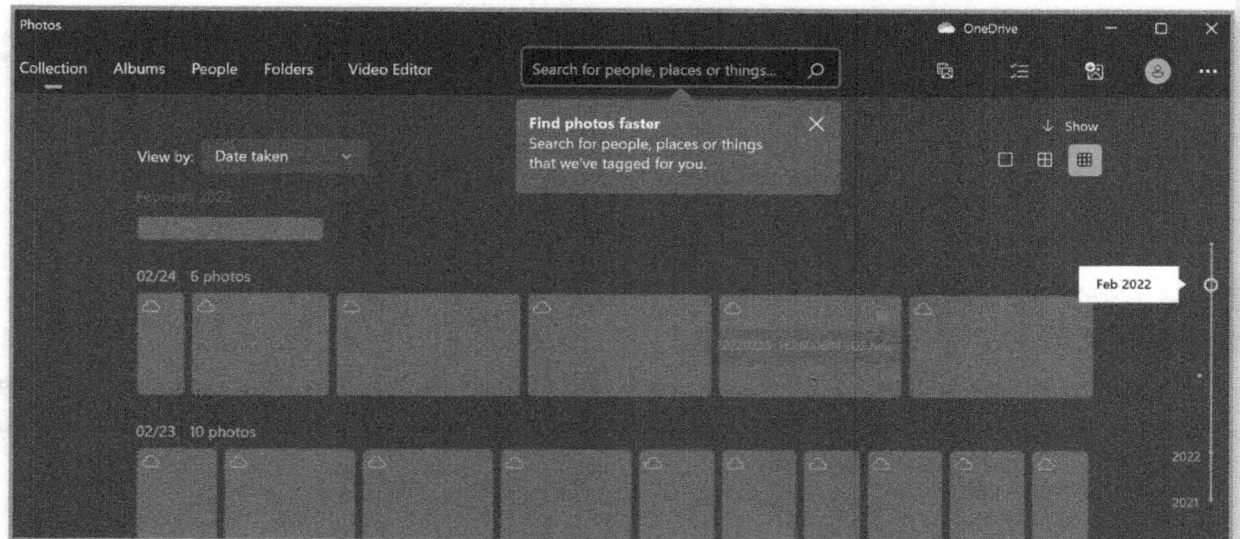

_ ☐ ✕

- **Open the Photos app by selecting it from the Apps list or typing 'Photos' into the ▨ Start menu.**

- In the Photos app, **select 'Import'** from the top right of the window.

- **Click on "Import from a device."**

- You may see a pop-up saying, "Something went wrong at this stage. **You need to ensure that your camera/tablet/smartphone is on and unlocked. Then click "Try again."**

- The Photos app will begin **"Looking for new photos and videos."** Give it a few minutes to carry out this task.

- Select which photos and videos you want to import and where you want them to be saved when this is complete.

   ♦ You can change the destination folder or create a new folder.

   ♦ **You can choose to import all the media or all the media you have captured since the last time you imported.** You can also use the checkboxes to handpick which photos and videos you want to import.

- Click the **'Import button'**, which should tell you how many files will be transferred to your computer.

_ □ ✕

- **Click OK to finish this process.**

- You can now find your photos and videos in the file you chose.

VIEWING DETAILS

You can see important details about a photo or video, such as its size, date of capture, file format, information about the device it was captured on, and even location data, if applicable, in the Photos app.

- **Select the image or video you want to investigate.**

- From the toolbar at the top of the window, **click on the Information icon shown with an 'i.'**

- An information pane will open on the right side showing all the details for the photo or video.

EDITING PICTURES

You can carry out many alterations to your photos using the Photos app.

- Select the **"Edit image"** button from the toolbar.

- An editing toolbar will open, showing Crop, Adjustment, Filter, and Markup options.

    ♦ The **CROP TOOL** is for resizing and removing unwanted parts of an image.

    ♦ Use the **ADJUSTMENT TOOL** to change lighting settings like brightness and contrast, color settings like saturation, and remove red-eye from your pictures.

    ♦ The **FILTER TOOL** offers a range of filters you can apply to your images, altering the shade and colors to give it the desired look and feel.

    ♦ The **MARKUP TOOL** can add annotations, drawings, and text to your photos.

21°C
Sunny intervals

12:00 AM
01/01/2022

_ ☐ ✕

- **Use the "Save as copy" button to save your new creation.** You can click the drop-down menu and choose 'Save' to overwrite the original image, saving only the version with your changes and edits.

CREATE A PHOTO ALBUM

Digital photo albums are collections of photos and videos from specific dates, special occasions, or related to particular themes like pets, people, scenery, etc.

The 🖼 Photo app will auto-create albums for you, but you can also create and customize your albums.

- **Create a new digital album by clicking on the button on the right side of the toolbar.** You will see a drop-down menu with options for:

  ◊ **NEW VIDEO PROJECT**
  ◊ **AUTOMATIC VIDEO**
  ◊ **IMPORT BACKUP**
  ◊ **ALBUM**

- **Select 'Album.'** Select all the photos and videos you want to include in your album using the checkboxes.

- **When you are finished, click on the 'Create' button** on the right side of the toolbar.

- **You will find your Albums by selecting 'Albums' from the toolbar.**

CREATING A SLIDESHOW

You can arrange your pictures into a slideshow to enjoy all the special moments.

- Open the Photos app and navigate to the folder with the pictures you would like to see in a slideshow.

- **At the top of the window, click on the button with three dots, and then select 'Slideshow' from the drop-down menu.**

_ □ ✕

- A slideshow will automatically start, showing all the pictures in the selected folder.

You can also use the video editor to create a slideshow using images instead of videos. Add photos into a new video project, and then arrange the order of the pictures in the Storyboard section.

You can adjust the amount of time each image is displayed, add a title card, and even background music to accompany the slideshow.

AUTOMATIC VIDEO

The  Photos app has intelligent software that can curate your photos and videos and select a few to produce unique videos just for you.

To create one of these automatic videos, **click on the "New video" button** on the right side of the toolbar and **select "Automatic video."**

EDITING VIDEOS

You can edit and even create videos using the new Photos app in Windows 11.

- **Open the  Photos app and click "Video editor" from the toolbar at the top of the window.**

- You will see a Project library on the left, a preview on the right, and a storyboard pane on the bottom.

- Select the video or videos you want to include by pressing the 'Add' button in the Project library section.

- A toolbar with several editing tools is at the top of the Storyboard pane. **Click on the video you want to edit to use these tools:**

    ◊ You can add a title card to the beginning of your video.
    ◊ Trim the length of the video.
    ◊ Split the video into different sections.
    ◊ Add text to the video.
    ◊ Change the motion and positioning of the video.
    ◊ Add 3D effects.

21°C
Sunny intervals

12:00 AM
01/01/2022

_ ☐ ✕

- ◊ Add filters.
- ◊ Change the speed.
- ◊ Crop the video.
- ◊ Undo the last action.
- ◊ Delete this video from the project.

At the top of the Video editor window, you will see a pencil icon that you can use to rename your project. You can also add background music or custom audio from your File Explorer. **You can also export the video in different formats by clicking "Finish video."**

FACIAL RECOGNITION

The  Photos app can employ sophisticated facial recognition software to identify friends and family members in your photos and videos. You can use this feature to create collections of specific people.

Click on 'People' in the toolbar to turn on this feature. Click 'Yes' to allow facial recognition. The feature will run in the background and create different groups based on the faces. You can rename the groups to match the person's name by right-clicking the collection and selecting 'rename.'

ADDING FAVORITES

Add pictures to your 'Favorites' collection so that you can always see your memorable photos and videos in the same place.

To mark images and videos as favorites, click on them and press the heart button on the toolbar. You can also right-click on images and select "Add to favorites." You can find your Favorites in the Album section.

🔍 PRINTING PHOTOS

You can print full-color photos on various paper types, including photo paper with glossy finishes, if you have a printer that can do this. Before proceeding, make sure your printer is connected correctly and turned on.

_ □ ✕

USING THE PHOTOS APP

- **Open the Photos app and click the picture you would like to print.**

- **Click on the button with three dots in the toolbar.**

- **Select Print** from the drop-down menu.

- Select your printer settings, such as which printer, how many copies, image quality and resolution, and how you want the image to be laid out and scaled with the page.

- **Click Print to send your pictures to the printer.**

USING FILE EXPLORER

- **Find the picture you want to print in** 🗀 **File Explorer.**

- **Right-click and select Print.**

- Select the correct printer, paper size, image quality, color, and layout options in the Print Dialogue.

- **Click on Print to send the image to the printer.**

🔍 SCANNING PHOTOS AND DOCUMENTS

If your printer can make copies, then it can also scan documents and save them onto your computer.

SCANNING APP AND SCANNER

The easiest way to scan a photo or document using a scanner is with the **Windows Scan app.**

- **Download the Windows Scan app from the** ⊞ **Microsoft Store.**

21°C
Sunny intervals

12:00 AM
01/01/2022

- **Once the app is installed, open it up.**

- **You will find some printer/scanner options, the file format you want your scan to be saved as, the color mode, page size, and which folder in which you would like the scan to be saved:**

  - Some printers have feeders and flatbeds; many only have flatbeds. A scanner with a feeder can scan both sides of a page while you need to flip the page over when using a flatbed manually.

- **Hit the 'Scan' button** at the bottom when you have set all of these options.

- **The scanner will import your file and save it in the specified location.**

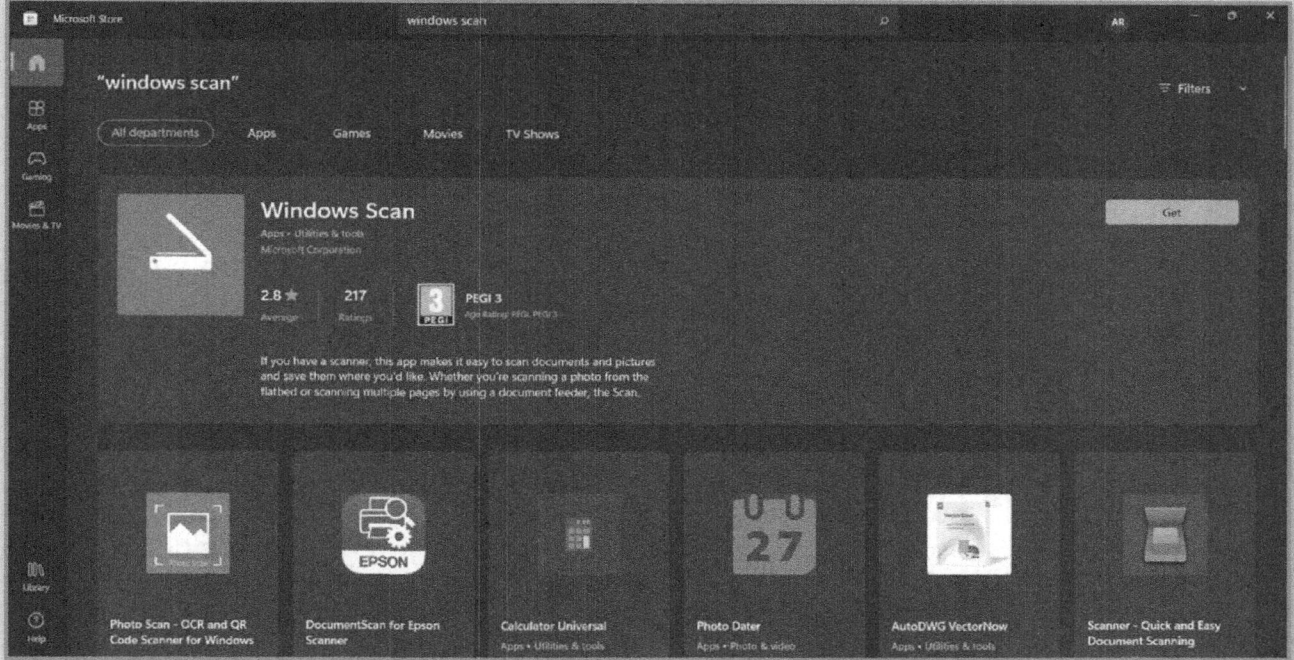

MICROSOFT LENS

Another way to scan content and save it onto your computer is to use the Microsoft Lens app. This is for mobile devices like smartphones and tablets that have cameras built-in.

_ □ ✕

- **Download Microsoft Lens from the**  **Microsoft Store** or Google Play Store. Ensure you download the correct app by checking that Microsoft Inc publishes it.

- Once the app is downloaded onto your mobile device, open it up.

- **You may need to grant access to the app to use your camera and access your files and media.**

- The app will then open your camera.

- Point it to the document or image you want to scan. When it is in the frame, hit the 'Capture' button.

- The next step is to properly adjust the borders to fit the image or document's corners. You can drag the tabs shown to adjust these borders.

- **When you are done, hit the 'Confirm' button.**

- You will see a scan of your photo or document, and you can make adjustments using the options provided, such as crop or filters.

- **You can also add multiple pages or images using the 'Add' button.**

- **When you have finished scanning, select the 'Done' button and input a name for the scan and the file format you want it to be saved as.** You can then pick a location where it will be saved.

- If your mobile device runs Windows 11, the files will reflect what you can see on your PC. However, if you run on a different operating system like Android or iOS, you can select the scan and send it to your Microsoft email address, where it can be downloaded.

- The Microsoft Lens app lets you choose what kind of media you want to scan and adjusts its settings to capture the highest quality image. In the capture screen, you can select Actions, Document, Whiteboard, Business Card or Photo.

21°C Sunny intervals   12:00 AM 01/01/2022

CHAPTER 10:

HAVING FUN
WITH WINDOWS 11

_ □ ×

Get the most out of your Windows 11 computer by taking full advantage of all the games, apps, and media capabilities it has to offer.

🔍 GAMING IMPROVEMENTS

GAME MODE

Windows 11 comes with several features that create a superior gaming experience. One of these changes is the Game Mode, which can be activated in the Settings app under the Gaming section.

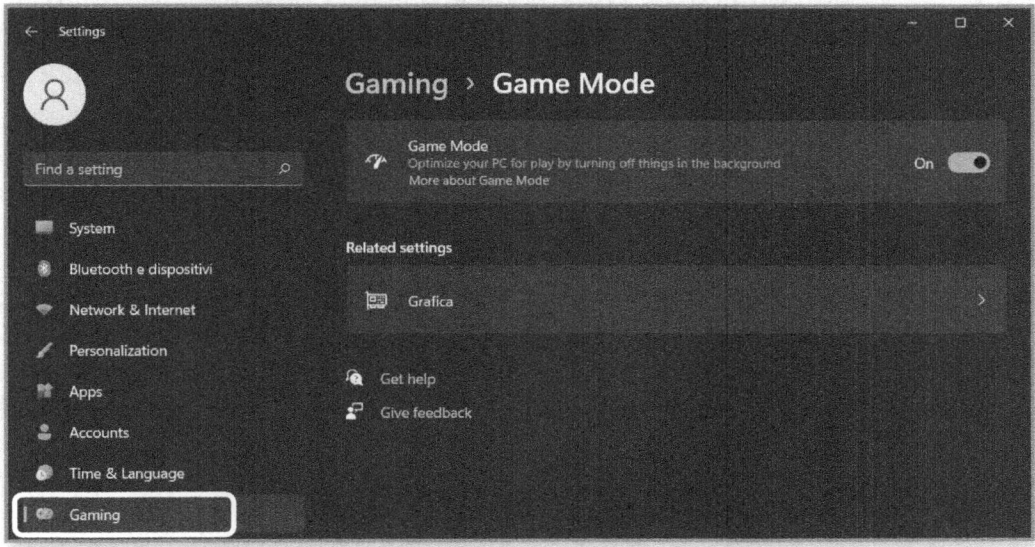

Game Mode helps optimize gameplay by reducing the number of processes running in the background.

XBOX GAME PASS

The Xbox app comes preinstalled on your Windows 11 computer, allowing you to sync data across your Xbox console and PC seamlessly. You also get access to the Xbox **Game Pass**, a subscription-based service that gives you unlimited access to more than 100 different games at an affordable price. With the Game Pass, you can get access to an expansive gaming library with some of the most critically-acclaimed gaming titles and Xbox exclusives. You can also browse for new games on a mobile device and choose to download them directly to your PC and Xbox console.

DIRECTX 12

DirectX 12 comes standard with Windows 11 computers. This is a piece of software that improves and optimizes communication between your computer's hardware, including the graphics cards, allowing for superior graphic effects and visuals. It helps highly-detailed games to run smoother and faster.

AUTO HDR

This feature comes standard with Xbox consoles but is now also included in Windows 11 PCs. **Auto HDR is an algorithm that converts SDR** (standard dynamic range) **games into HDR** (high dynamic range). It helps to improve the appearance of the graphics and visuals, giving them brighter and more vibrant colors and images.

DIRECTSTORAGE

Loading times in games is one of the most significant downsides of PC gaming, but with DirectStorage, your Windows 11 PC can drastically reduce these delays. **DirectStorage allows the GPU** (graphics processing unit) **to improve and accelerate the data transfer speeds of the CPU** (central processing unit) **by taking over some of these tasks.**

_ □ ✕

ANDROID GAMES

Windows 11 PCs are compatible with all of your favorite games and apps that typically run on your Android smartphone. You can find all of this content in the Microsoft Store or the Amazon Webstore, including your social media apps such as Facebook, Instagram, and TikTok, as well as mobile gaming classics like Candy Crush, Subway Surfers, Clash of Clans, and more.

🔍 WHAT GAMES CAN I PLAY?

You will be able to continue playing almost all of the games that ran on the previous operating system, Windows 10. However, older games designed to work on Windows 8, 7, or older operating systems may no longer be supported on Windows 11.

On Windows 11, you can access games through various digital gaming storefronts and downloaders such as Steam, Origin, the Epic Games Store, and the Microsoft Store.

NATIVE GAMES

Windows operating systems have a long history of including games in their products. Some of the most nostalgic titles include Minesweeper, Solitaire, 3D Pinball, and Hearts. Most of these games have been phased out, and **Windows 11 is only compatible with the Solitaire Collection, which includes Classic Solitaire, Spider Solitaire, and FreeCell.** These are all card games that follow the same rules as their real-life namesakes.

To download and install the Solitaire Collection, open the 🗔 **Microsoft Store by clicking the app icon in your app list or type it into the** ⊞ **Start menu.** Search for the Solitaire Collection and click the Install button. You can launch the game by clicking Play.

Once the game is running, you can make it easier to access by pinning it to your taskbar or Start menu. Right-click on the game icon found on the taskbar and select "Pin to taskbar" or "Pin to Start."

_ ☐ ✕

🔍 EXPLORING THE MICROSOFT STORE

The Microsoft App Store is your go-to app for downloading all the apps and games you need. It is the safest way to download content onto your PC and will not run the risk of infecting your computer with viruses or malware like you may get when downloading content from an internet browser.

The Microsoft Store also offers a new 'pop-up' store that will appear if you browse the internet for apps and games. If the app or game is available for download through the Microsoft Store, you will see a pop-up where you can click download. This enables the Microsoft Store to manage the download and installation process rather than the internet browser.

_ ☐ ✕

MANAGE MICROSOFT STORE ACCOUNT SETTINGS

To use all the features offered in the Microsoft Store, you will need to sign in using your Microsoft Account. To view these settings, click on your profile picture found to the

21°C
Sunny intervals

12:00 AM
01/01/2022

right of the search bar. **Click "Manage account and devices."** Here you will be able to see all of your apps, devices, and accounts, and you can view, cancel and renew subscriptions or unlink any devices.

PAYMENTS

Find and edit your payment information by clicking on your profile picture to the right of the search bar and selecting "Payment methods." This is where you can add your debit card, credit card, bank account, PayPal account, or mobile phone as a payment method for the Microsoft Store.

When purchasing a game or app, you will be able to choose between any of these methods to complete the checkout, and the Microsoft Store will ensure a safe and reliable transfer of funds. You will be able to see all of your previous transactions in this section as well.

REDEEMING CODES

If you have a gift card or discount code for the Microsoft Store, you can input it by clicking on your profile picture to the right of the search bar and selecting the option for "Redeem code or gift cards."

Gift cards can be used on any app, game, or content on the Microsoft Store, and you can buy them online, in stores, or through the Microsoft Store itself. They offer credits or discounts. The Gift Cards will provide you with a 25-digit code that you input into the space provided. Codes work in the same way.

You can use your discounts or credits when purchasing games. You will be asked if you want to use your Gift Card or code or if you want to use one of your other payment methods at checkout.

APP SETTINGS

The app settings can also be accessed by clicking on your profile picture to the left of the search bar. You will see settings for app updates, sign-in options, offline permissions, and video autoplay.

_ □ X

NAVIGATING THE MICROSOFT STORE

Upon opening the **Microsoft Store app**, you will see the home screen showing some of the most popular or trending apps and games available for purchase and download. There is a search bar across the top of the window and a navigation bar on the left with buttons:

- **Home -** the main storefront, showing featured apps, games, and notable collections.

- **Apps -** where you can find some of the most popular, highest rated, and featured apps to meet any need you can think of.

- **Gaming -** an area dedicated to all kinds of games, including arcade, adventure, puzzle, and simulation games. You can find a range of free and pay-to-play games as well as those included in your Xbox Game Pass.

- **Movies & TV -** get access to all of the best streaming services, including Netflix, Amazon Prime Video, Disney+, Hulu, and more. You can find specific shows, series, and movies through the Microsoft Store, and it will direct you to the streaming service that hosts the content.

- **Library -** this is where you can find all your downloaded apps, games, movies, TV shows, and more.

- **Help -** get assistance with any problems you experience when navigating the Microsoft Store.

To find a game, you can type the name into the search bar or look through some Microsoft Store recommendations to discover new and exciting content to keep you entertained. Games will be recommended to you based on your previous downloads, and you can also find different categories and genres to search through, depending on your interests.

Click on the game that you want to download. You will be directed to the game's page, where you can find additional information such as descriptions, ratings, and reviews. You can also see the cost of the game though many will be free for download.

Click the 'Get' button or the price to download and install a game. The Microsoft Store will run these processes for you in the background, and when the game is ready to play, you can press the 'Launch' button.

21°C
Sunny intervals

12:00 AM
01/01/2022

_ ☐ ✕

SEARCHING

When typing anything into the **Search Bar**, the Microsoft Store will try to narrow the results for you. When you hit Enter, you can select which store department you want to narrow your search to. **You can click "All departments," 'Apps,' 'Games,' 'Movies,' or "TV Shows."**

There is also a 'Filters' button on the left side that you can use to specify your search details, such as the content's intended age range, category, subscription service, and cost. If you only want to see free games, you can use the filter to narrow your search results.

MANAGING YOUR LIBRARY

The Library tab is where you can stay on top of all the apps, games, and other content that you have downloaded onto your PC through the Microsoft Store. You will be able to see content that is busy downloading or updating and all of the games and apps already installed. You can also see games or apps you have downloaded onto other devices you have signed into using your Microsoft account. These are indicated with a small cloud icon.

You can download these apps or games onto your current device by clicking this cloud icon, and all of the existing data will also be synced. For example, if you have downloaded a game onto a mobile device but would also like to play the game on your PC, all of your game progress, such as levels passed and awards, will be synced onto your PC.

The Library is also where you will ensure all of your games and apps are kept up to date. **Click the "Get updates" button on the top right side of the window, and the Microsoft Store will scan all of your apps for any available updates.** These will be automatically downloaded and installed so that you can always play the latest versions.

HOW TO UNINSTALL AN APP OR GAME

There are two main ways to remove and uninstall any app or game from your Windows 11 device:

1. The first way is to **use the** ▦ **Start menu:**

_ □ ✕

- **Open the ▪ Start menu and click "All Apps"** from the top right corner
- Scroll down the list and find the app which you want to remove
- **Right-click and select "Uninstall.'**
- Confirm your choice by clicking 'Uninstall' in the pop-up window
- This method will work for most apps, but some may require additional steps:

  ◊ Clicking 'Uninstall' on some apps, such as VLC, will open up the Control Panel to the "Programs and Features" section.
  ◊ You will see a list of programs, find the one you want to uninstall again, and click on it.
  ◊ Then click on the 'Uninstall' button at the top of the list.
  ◊ **You can also use this Control Panel method to uninstall any game or program on your computer.**

2. Another way to uninstall an app or game is to **use ⚙ Settings:**

- **Open the ⚙ Settings app**
- Navigate to **APPS > APPS & FEATURES**
- Find the app you want to uninstall from the list
- **Click the button with three dots** on the right side of the app's name
- **Select 'Uninstall'**

🔍 LISTEN TO MUSIC AND WATCH VIDEOS

There are so many ways you can listen to music on your Windows 11 computer. You can use streaming services like Spotify or use a media player to listen to CDs or mp3s already on your computer.

MUSIC STREAMING - SPOTIFY

You can download the Spotify app from the ▪ Microsoft Store.
Once installed, open the app and begin the sign-in process by entering your password and email address, or you can sign up for a brand new account.

21°C
Sunny intervals

12:00 AM
01/01/2022

You can sign into the same Spotify account using multiple devices, allowing you to carry your music and playlists with you wherever you go.

Navigate the Spotify app using the buttons down the left side:

- **BROWSE -** find new songs, artists, and genres to listen to

- **RADIO -** allow Spotify to create a custom playlist based on a song, album, playlist, or artist that you have selected.

- **YOUR MUSIC -** find your recently played songs, songs, albums, artists, and stations that you have liked. You can also find Local files, where you can find downloaded content for listening offline.

- **PLAYLISTS -** this is where you can find your favorite playlists and Spotify's playlists that feature new music.

In the middle part of the app, you can browse and discover new music or listen to your favorites. **Use the search bar at the top to find specific tracks, artists, or albums.**

Use the player at the bottom of the app to pause, skip, adjust volume, and shuffle settings.

Add friends who will appear on the right side of the app and see what they are listening to. You can also share your music with your friends.

SPOTIFY PREMIUM

The free version of Spotify grants you access to the entire music and podcast library, but you may be interrupted regularly by ads. The free version also prevents you from downloading content so that you can listen offline.

To take full advantage of the app's features, you will need to subscribe to Spotify Premium by following these steps:

- **Visit www.spotify.com** and log in using your email address/username and password.
- **Select 'Upgrade' in the menu bar.**
- Select what kind of membership and price point you would like to pay for.
- Enter your payment information
- **Refresh your desktop app**, and you will now have access to **Spotify Premium.**

GROOVE MUSIC AND WINDOWS MEDIA PLAYER

Both of these apps come standard with Windows 11 and can play most media files. You can use them to listen to music and create playlists. You can find either app by typing their name into the Start menu.

The main difference between the two is that Groove Music can be installed on multiple devices and will sync your songs, artists, albums, and playlists across these devices so that you can listen to your music wherever you go.

VLC MEDIA

VLC is a third-party media player that can be used to view or listen to almost any kind of media file, including videos, music, podcasts, and more. It is a very simple to use and easy-to-understand app.

To load media into VLC, find the content in File Explorer and drag it directly into the open VLC app window

21°C
Sunny intervals

12:00 AM
01/01/2022

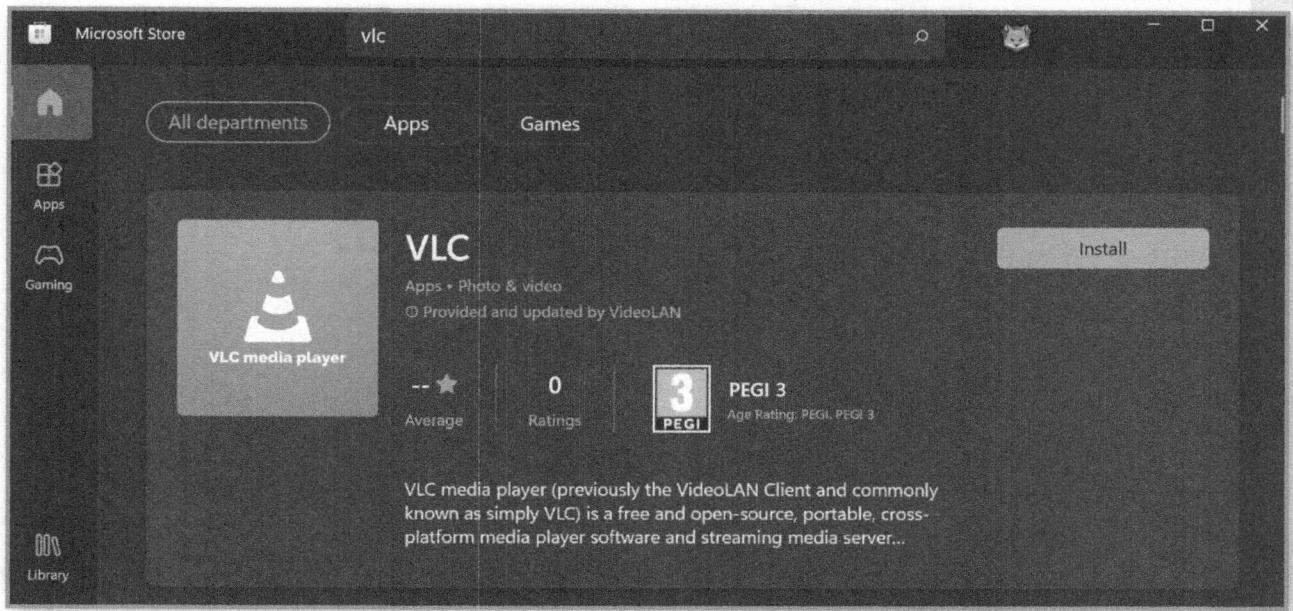

Download VLC from Microsoft Store
(see more details on page 74)

CHAPTER 11:

TIPS AND TRICKS

Get the most out of your Windows 11 experience by learning some of the most useful tips and tricks.

TROUBLESHOOTING

BOOTING IN SAFE MODE

If your computer has problems starting up correctly, experiences crashes, or has issues running software; you can try using Safe Mode to help diagnose or narrow down the exact cause. In Safe Mode, your Windows PC will start up in a basic and limited state. If your computer is having issues, but it can run properly in Safe Mode, it means that the problem is not caused by Windows' basic settings or drivers and is probably related to something else you have installed.

There are two main versions of Safe Mode: Safe Mode and Safe Mode with Networking. You will know you have booted up in Safe Mode correctly if you can see the words "Safe Mode" on the bottom right of your desktop, above the time and date.

There are a few ways to enter Safe Mode. Make sure to follow the instructions carefully and begin with the first option before moving on to the next:

1. Open the ⚙ **SETTINGS APP > SYSTEM > RECOVERY**

2. Under Advanced startup, click **"Restart now."**

21°C
Sunny intervals

12:00 AM
01/01/2022

_ □ ✕

3. **Your PC will restart and display the Recovery menu that says "Choose an option."**

4. **Click TROUBLESHOOT > ADVANCED OPTIONS > STARTUP SETTINGS > RESTART**

5. **Your PC will restart**, and you will be given a list of options to choose from

6. **Press F4 or 4 on your keyboard to enter Safe Mode, or press F5 or 5 to enter Safe Mode with Networking, enabling your system to access the internet.**

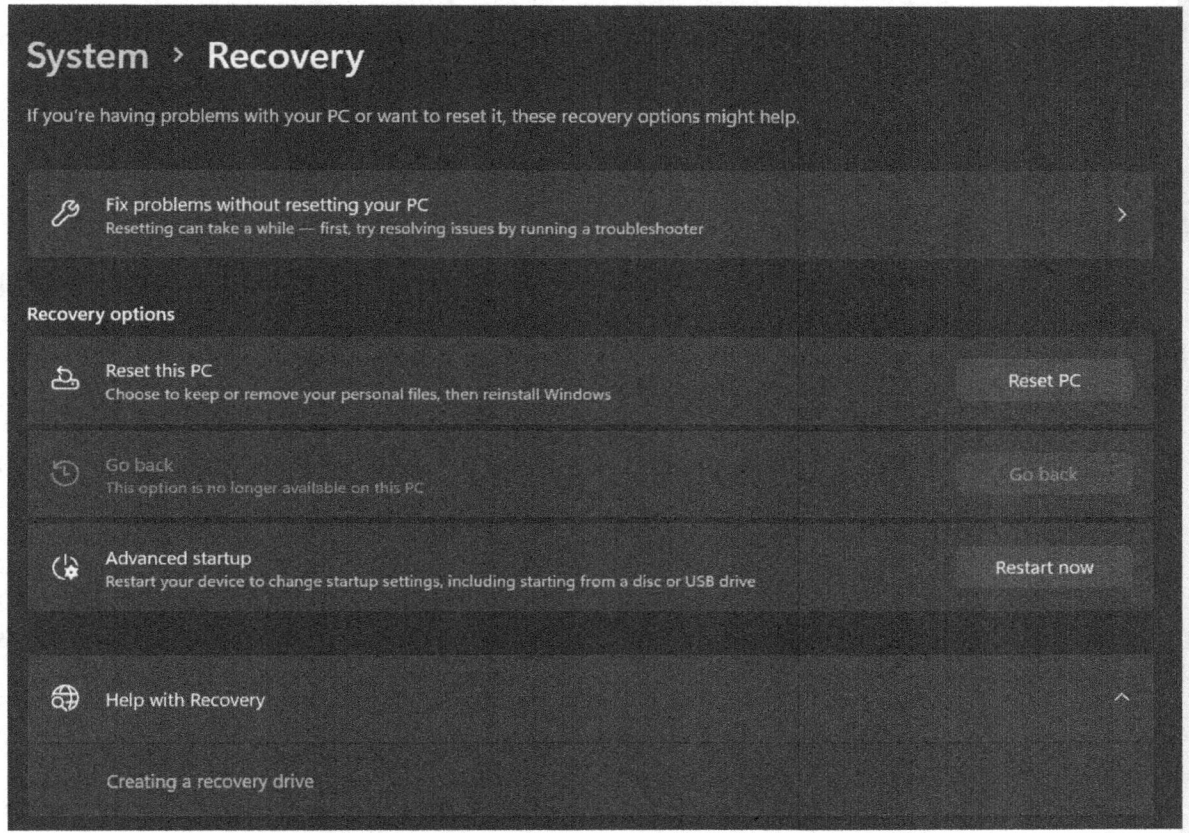

_ □ ✕

FROM THE SIGN-IN SCREEN

If you are having trouble opening the Settings app, you can follow these steps instead:
- Restart your device

_ □ ✕

- **When you see the sign-in screen, press and hold down the Shift key while selecting Power > Restart**

- **Your PC will restart** to the Recovery menu that says **"Choose an option."**

- Now you can follow the same steps mentioned previously:

- Click **TROUBLESHOOT > ADVANCED OPTIONS > STARTUP SETTINGS > RESTART**

- **Your PC will restart**, and you will be given a list of options to choose from

- **Press F4 or 4 on your keyboard to enter Safe Mode, or press F5 or 5 to enter Safe Mode with Networking, enabling your system to access the internet.**

FROM A BLANK SCREEN

For more severe problems that prevent your operating system from starting up properly, preventing you from gaining access to the sign-in screen or settings app, you will need **to force your device to enter the Windows Recovery Environment** (WinRE) by repeatedly turning it on and off following these steps:

- **Hold down the power button on your device for 10 seconds to force a shutdown.**

- Press the power button again **to turn the device on**

- Wait for Windows to begin running; you will see the manufacturer's logo appear on the screen. **Hold down the power button for 10 seconds to turn the device off again when you see this.**

- Press the power button **to turn your device back on**

- Wait for Windows to begin running. **Once again, hold down the power button for 10 seconds when you see the manufacturer's logo.**

- **Turn the device back on by pressing the power button.**

- **Your device should now start up in Automatic Repair mode.**

- **Select Advanced options to enter WinRE.**

- Now you can follow the same steps as mentioned previously:

21°C
Sunny intervals

12:00 AM
01/01/2022

_ □ ✕

- **CLICK TROUBLESHOOT > ADVANCED OPTIONS > STARTUP SETTINGS > RESTART**

- **Your PC will restar**t, and you will be given a list of options to choose from

- **Press F4 or 4 on your keyboard to enter Safe Mode, or press F5 or 5 to enter Safe Mode with Networking, enabling your system to access the internet.**

WHAT TO DO IN SAFE MODE

Once your PC has booted up in Safe Mode, you can begin troubleshooting and identifying the cause of the problem.

- **Scan for viruses or malware:**

  - ♦ **Open ⚙ SETTINGS > PRIVACY & SECURITY > WINDOWS SECURITY**

  - ♦ **Click "Quick scan"** to search your computer for threats.

- **Uninstall recently installed software:**

  - ♦ **Open ⚙ SETTINGS > APPS > APP LIST**

  - ♦ **Navigate to your recently installed apps and right-click to uninstall them**

You can try a few other options in Safe Mode, but it may permanently alter your operating system's files, and you should consult with Microsoft Support first.

LEAVING SAFE MODE

When you have finished working in Safe Mode, all you need to do is shut down your device and start it back up again. It will start up Windows 11 in regular mode.

SEE HOW MUCH SPACE YOU HAVE ON YOUR PC

The amount of storage available on your computer is determined by the size of your hard drive. You need storage space for your operating system and all its related content, as well as all your additional apps, programs, and files. Your computer will also use some

_ □ ✕

storage space to run processes.

- You can see how much space is available by opening ⚙ **SETTINGS > SYSTEM > STORAGE.**

- **The first thing you will see is the Local Disk (C:).** This is your hard drive. You can see how big it is and how much space is currently being used by your computer.

- Below your Local Disk, you will see other categories using the most space. This may include **Temporary files or Apps & Features.**

- Click on the **"Show more categories"** button to see more, including System & reserved, Other people, Documents, Pictures, Other, etc.

- If you click on one of these categories, such as Apps & features, you can see a further breakdown of how much space each of your installed apps uses.

- **If you have more than one hard drive installed on your PC, you can view information for these by clicking STORAGE MANAGEMENT > ADVANCED STORAGE SETTINGS > STORAGE used on other drives.**

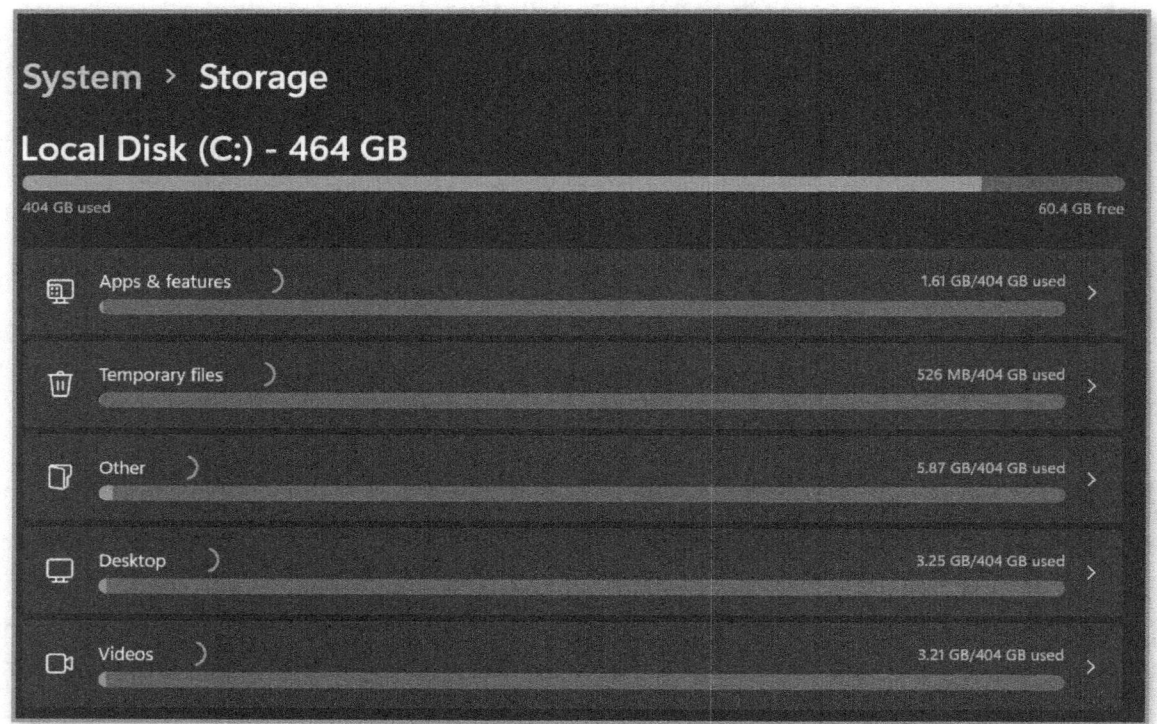

21°C
Sunny intervals

12:00 AM
01/01/2022

_ ☐ ✕

DELETING TEMPORARY FOLDERS

Temporary files are created to store data and progress while you are busy working on a permanent file.

They are stored in **C:\USERS\APPDATA\LOCAL\TEMP** with the .TMP file extension (**you can also search in the finder, the following words "%temp%".** See the printscreen).

They are useful and can help your computer run faster and smoothly while working on a large project, but when you are finished, they can take up a lot of space and make your PC slower.

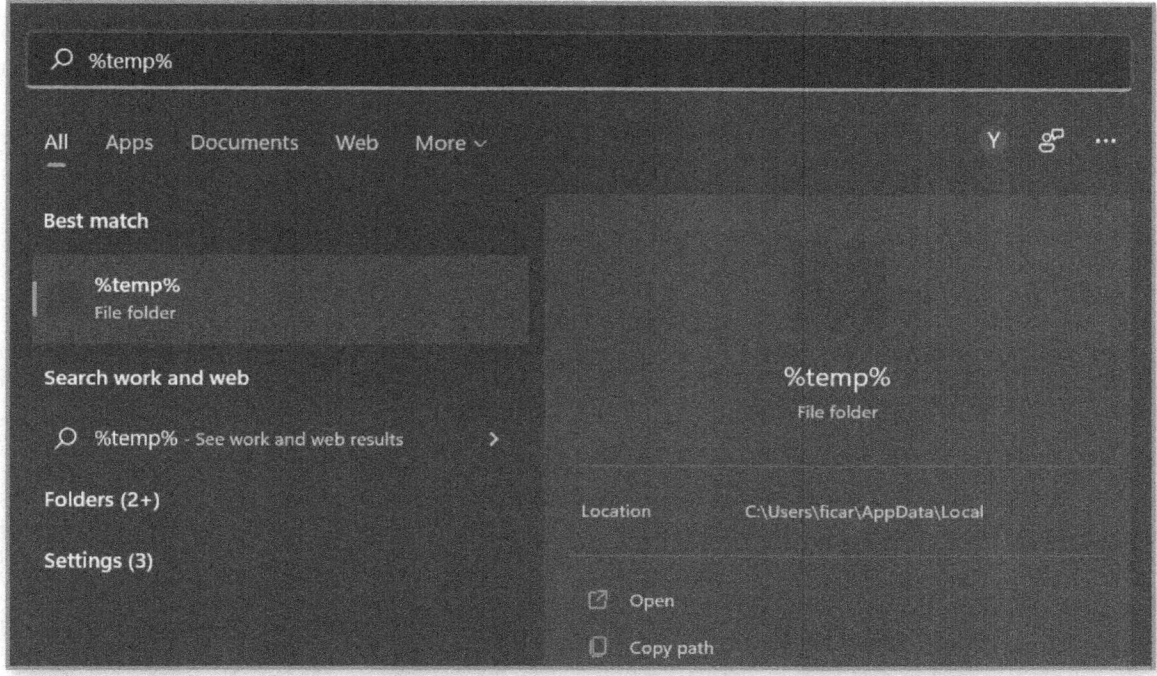

_ ☐ ✕

To remove temporary files:
- **Open folder "%temp%"**
- **Select all files in the folder with CTRL + A**
- **Delete with "canc"**
- **Click on "skip" if there will be some files that can't be deleted**

_ □ X

You can also:
- **Open the Settings app > System > Storage > Local Disk**
- **Click "Temporary files."**
- **Select the temporary files you want to remove using the checkboxes.**

  ◊   Windows 11 will recommend which files you should delete and how big they are. It will not display files that are important for proper system functioning.

- **Click the "Remove files" button at the top of the list when you are done.**

You can also use **Storage Sense** which periodically deletes temporary files and clears the Recycle Bin:

- **Open ⚙ SETTINGS > SYSTEM > STORAGE > STORAGE MANAGEMENT**
- **Toggle the switch to turn "Storage Sense" on.**
- **Select 'Enable' when prompted**
- **Your PC will not scan for unnecessary files automatically.**
- You can configure how often you want these files to be cleared out.

Storage Sense can also be used to keep your Downloads library clean by removing old files.

THE SECRET START MENU

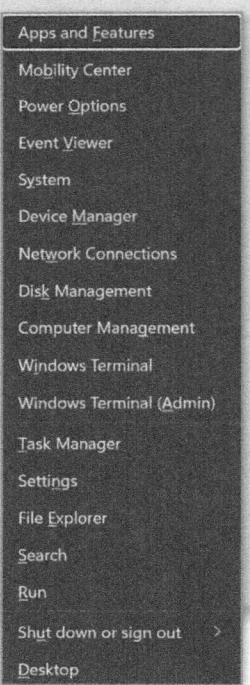

You can press the Windows key + X to access the secret Start menu, a simple pop-up menu with shortcuts to some essential administrative tools, and shut down options.

If you have a touchscreen device, you can bring up the menu by tapping and holding down the Start button.

The secret start menu allows you to quickly access your Installed apps, Power Options, Device Manager, Network Connections, Task Manager, Settings, File Explorer, Search, and more.

Using it can help to save you some time and clicks.

21°C
Sunny intervals

12:00 AM
01/01/2022

_ □ ✕

TAKE A SCREENSHOT OF SPECIFIC CONTENT

You have already learned some fundamental ways to take screenshots, including the PrtScr button on your keyboard and the clipping tool. However, you can also use the keyboard shortcut **Win+Shift+S.**

This will open the Snip tool, graying out the screen and allowing you to drag your mouse cursor over the area you want to capture. There are buttons along the top of the screen letting you choose between a rectangular snip, a freehand snip, a snip of your current window, or the entire screen.

HOW TO USE FOCUS ASSISTANT

Focus Assist is a tool that can help you minimize distractions while working on your PC. You can use it while completing an important document, in a meeting with colleagues, when watching a TV show or movie, or when you are struggling to beat a boss in one of your games. Focus Assist allows you to turn off all or some of your notifications. You can configure it only to display high-priority messages or notifications from specific contacts.

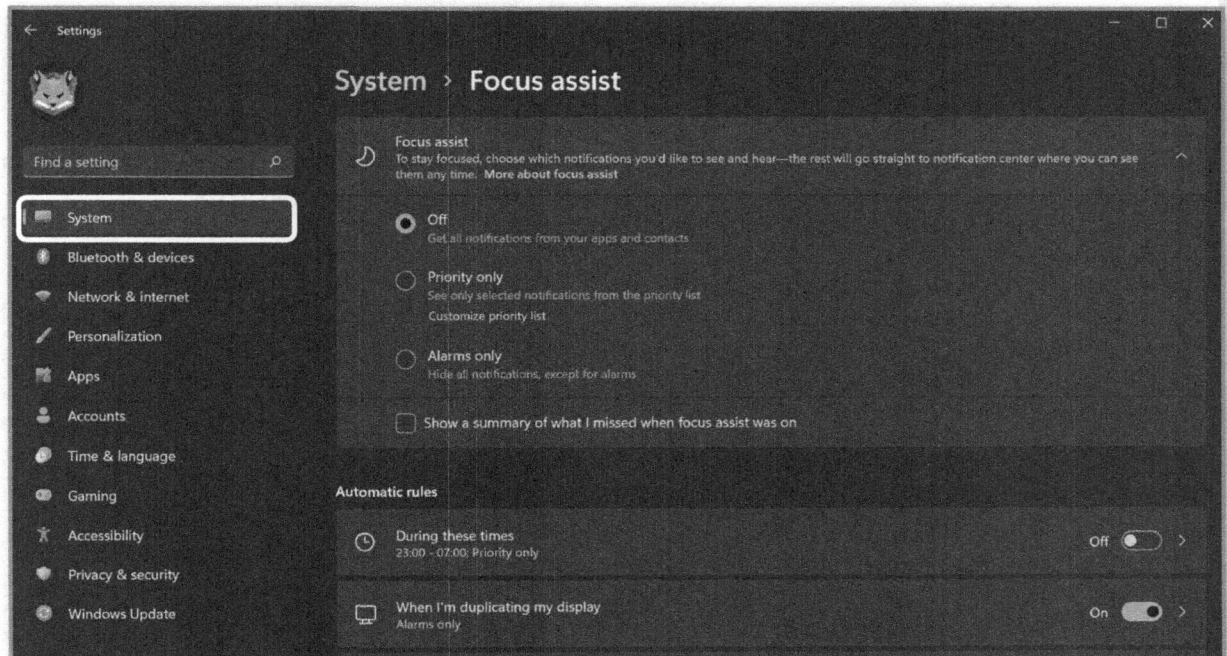

21°C
Sunny intervals

12:00 AM
01/01/2022

_ ☐ ✕

To turn on Focus Assistant or change the settings:

- Open ⚙ **SETTINGS > SYSTEM > FOCUS ASSIST.**
- **Select Off, Priority only, or Alarms only.**
- **Click "Customize priority list":**

  ◇ Choose if you want to receive calls, texts, and reminders using the checkboxes.
  ◇ Add specific contacts you want to receive notifications from under the People section.
  ◇ Add apps to receive notifications from under the Apps section.

- Click the checkbox if you want Focus Assist to prepare a list of all the notifications and alarms you missed while it was enabled.
- **You can also set Automatic Rules for Focus Assist:**

  ◇ Set specific times in which Focus Assist will turn on
  ◇ Choose what happens when working with a duplicate display
  ◇ Enable Focus Assist when playing games
  ◇ Configure settings for full-screen mode
  ◇ Reduce notifications after a Windows update

REALIGN THE START BUTTON

If you are unhappy with the redesigned taskbar and placement of the Start menu, you can return to tradition and align it back to the left side of the Desktop.

Right-click anywhere on the taskbar that is blank and then click "Taskbar settings."

The ⚙ **Settings app** will open on the Taskbar section under **PERSONALIZATION.** Scroll to Taskbar behaviors and find the option for Taskbar alignment. **Change 'Center' to 'Left'**

Your taskbar and Start menu will now be aligned to the left side of your screen.

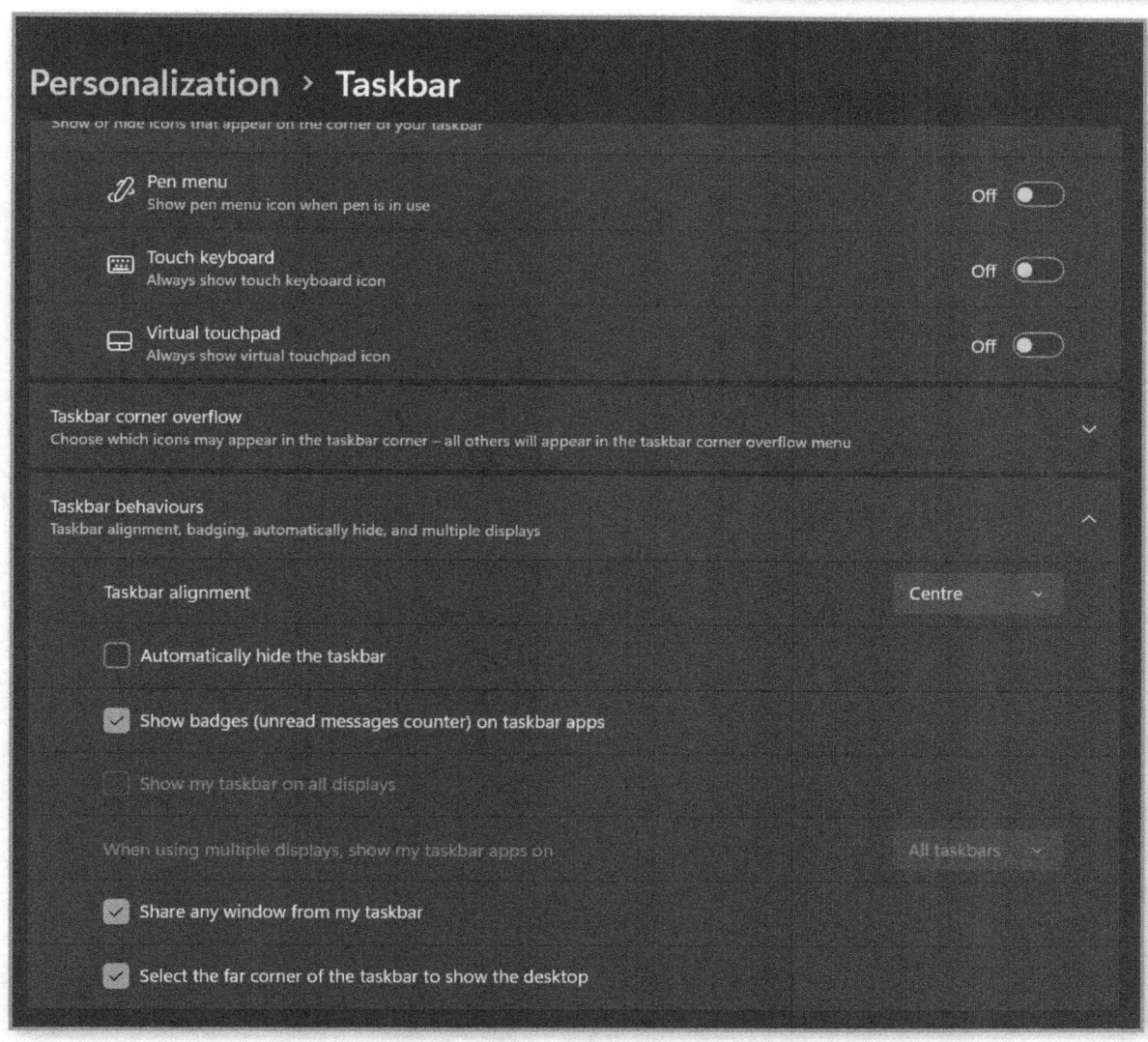

JUMP TO DESKTOP

You can instantly minimize all of your open windows and jump to a view of your Desktop using the keyboard shortcut Win+D.

This is useful when working with many different windows or in full-screen mode, which is often used to play games. Your apps and windows will remain open, and you can restore them by clicking their icons in the taskbar.

SEE THE CLIPBOARD

When copying and pasting, it can be helpful to see the actual clipboard that your content is saved to. You can easily do this by using the keyboard shortcut Win+V.

The first time you use this feature, you will be asked to turn on Clipboard history. It will be disabled by default to reduce storage needs on your hard drive.

Once enabled, you will see a list showing everything that has been copied recently in a small clipboard window. Each copied item will be displayed in its own tab. Click on a tab to paste it into an active document instantly.

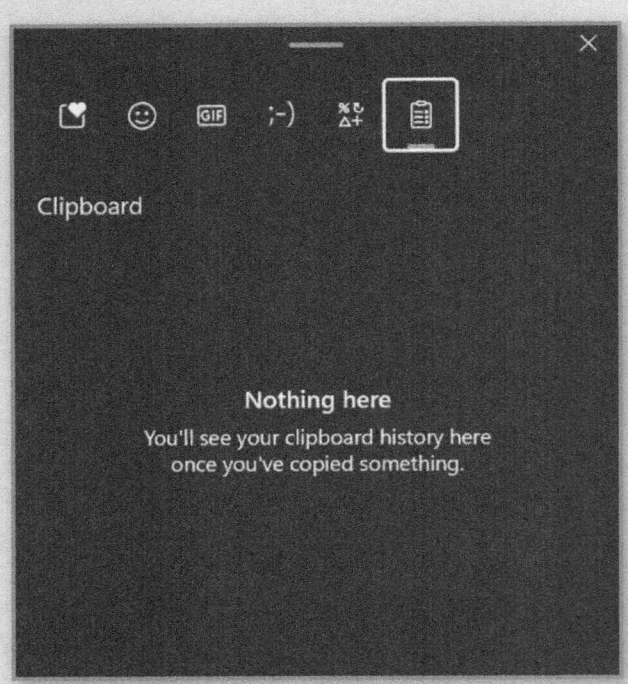

In addition to your copied content, you can also use the Clipboard to get emojis, animated GIFs, and special symbols to copy and paste into your documents or chats.

SOUND SETTINGS

Windows 11 offers many ways to customize your sound settings.

You can use multiple different output devices simultaneously while also setting different volumes for each of the apps you are using.

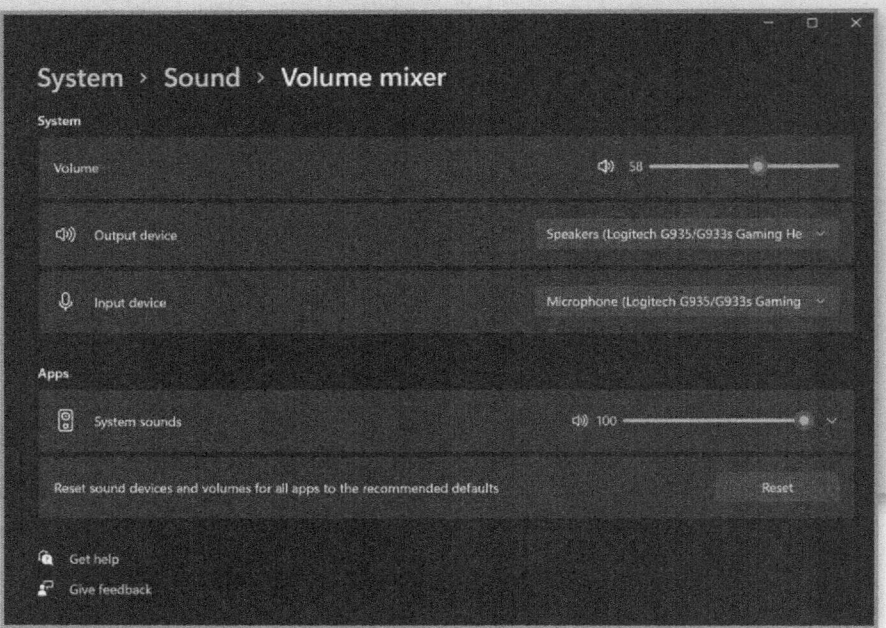

_ □ ✕

AUDIO OUTPUT

Decide whether you want sound to come out of your device's built-in speakers, external speakers, through the headphone jack, or a Bluetooth speaker or headset.

- Open ⚙ **SETTINGS > SYSTEM > SOUND > OUTPUT**
- Your connected devices will be displayed here for you to select.
- You can also pair a new device here using Bluetooth.

CHANGE APPLICATION VOLUMES

You can change the volume of specific apps:

- Open ⚙ **SETTINGS > SYSTEM > SOUND > ADVANCED**

- **Select "Volume mixer."**

- You will see a list of apps, and you can adjust the slider to set the desired volume for each app individually.

- You can also set which output device each app should use. For example, one app can produce sound through a Bluetooth headset, while another can produce sound through your device's built-in speakers.

VIEW YOUR BATTERY SETTINGS

Windows 11 allows you to see the power usage of your battery if you are using a mobile device like a laptop, tablet, or smartphone.

In ⚙ **SETTINGS > POWER & BATTERY,** you can see a graph showing your battery levels over time. You can also view a list that shows battery usage per app.

Use this feature to quickly identify which apps are guzzling the power and change these settings. Some settings that you can change include turning off background processes to only work when you have the app window open.

_ □ X

TOUCHPAD GESTURES

Get the most out of your touchpad or touch screen device by using the default gestures:

TAPPING: Use taps to click on or select content on your screen. You can use single saps for normal clicks and double tabs for right-clicks.

ZOOMING AND SCROLLING: Zoom in using your touchpad by pinching two fingers together, or zoom out by dragging your fingers away from each other. Scroll by swiping up or down on the scroll bar shown on the screen.

THREE-FINGERS: You can swipe with three fingers to scroll multiple pages at once, though you can also program your own custom functions in:

- ⚙ **SETTINGS > DEVICES > TOUCHPAD.**

21°C
Sunny intervals

12:00 AM
01/01/2022

CONCLUSION

_ ☐ ✕

Windows 11 is designed to be easy to use, with an intuitive organization system and attractive design. However, even a casual user will benefit from learning some tips and tricks so that their experience can run faster and more smoothly.

This title has covered many of the essentials that you need to work and play on a Windows 11 device confidently. You can appreciate how Windows has evolved and how some of the newest features have greatly expanded and transformed how people use their computers. You should be able to identify the hardware requirements needed to run the operating system and initiate the upgrade process when it becomes available to new devices.

Understanding File Explorer is one of the first and most critical steps to becoming a Windows 11 passionate. You should now know how to navigate and find your content, manage, organize, delete files, and curate your libraries to suit your specific needs. You can also rest assured knowing that you can use the Setting app to its full potential, from managing your Microsoft account, sign in options, customizing the taskbar, pinning apps, changing your scaling and resolution options, utilizing the various accessibility features, and customizing the appearance of your operating system to suit your personality. You should also be able to install any device, be it a scanner, Bluetooth device, or additional monitor.

The Windows Desktop is your port of call for all apps, programs, and windows. You can customize your background wallpaper, arrange icons and shortcuts, and even create virtual desktops. Moving and resizing windows is as easy as a click and drag, and with the addition of widgets in Windows 11, you can also display all the information you need to see without cluttering your display.

Installing new software has become much easier in Windows 11 than in the past. Make sure to utilize the Microsoft Store to get access to almost any app you can think of, and use your internet browser to find even more content. Ensure you only install verified and reviewed products to reduce your risk of infecting your PC with viruses or malware and find good antivirus software.

Using your web browsers, such as Google Chrome or Microsoft Edge, you can stay up to date with everything happening in the world around you.

_ □ X

From news updates to social media and entertainment services like YouTube. You will be able to create bookmarks to save all your important web pages and use the tab system like a pro.

Send your friends and family a surprise email just because you can! Using the Windows 11 Mail app, draft an exciting email and attach pictures so that your contacts can see all the things you have been getting up to lately. You can even include emojis or animated GIFs in your emails. Use the Mail and Calendar app to send out invitations for upcoming events or schedule a video call so that you can all chat in real-time.

Microsoft Teams can help make your video calls easy, efficient, and meaningful. Connect with people across the world and take recordings so that you can go back and reminisce in the future. You can also use Teams confidently to carry out work meetings, interviews, and even give presentations without needing to leave your home.

Don't forget to use some productivity apps to make your day-to-day life even more accessible. From the To-Do lists to Calendar to Maps. Make lists to keep you on top of all your tasks, schedule deadlines, and pre-plan your trips with live traffic data so that you are always on time. You can also create engaging documents using WordPad, with no need to pay for expensive Microsoft 365 subscriptions.

Use the updated Photos app to transform your media library. Sort, organize, and even edit your photos. Create slideshows and collections, so your memories are right there when you need them. The Photos app can also create and edit professional-quality videos that you can send to people using the Mail app.

Windows 11 has geared up to the next level of gaming as well. Explore the wide world of arcade, adventure, puzzle, shooter, and role-playing games on offer in the Microsoft Store and various game launchers.

Finally, you can awe your children and grandchildren with your tech-savvy use of Windows shortcuts, secret menus, customized sound settings, and troubleshooting abilities. You will never have to call them up to figure out a problem again.

21°C Sunny intervals   12:00 AM 01/01/2022

INDEX

I

J

K

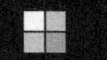   

21°C
Sunny intervals

12:00 AM
01/01/2022

21°C
Sunny intervals

12:00 AM
01/01/2022

21°C
Sunny intervals

12:00 AM
01/01/2022

REFERENCES

AnandK@TWC. (2021a, October 10). *Windows 11 Settings: How to open and use them to tweak your PC.* The Windows Club. https://www.thewindowsclub.com/open-and-use-windows-11-settings

AnandK@TWC. (2021b, October 25). *Best Windows 11 file explorer tips and tricks.* The Windows Club. https://www.thewindowsclub.com/windows-11-file-explorer-tips-and-tricks

Butler, S. (2022, February 10). *Why Windows 11 Is better for PC gaming than Windows 10.* How-to Geek. https://www.howtogeek.com/773799/why-windows-11-is-better-for-pc-gaming-than-windows-10/

Carrasqueira, J. (2021, July 7). *XDA Basics: How do I use Windows 11? A guide to the new OS.* Xda-Developers. https://www.xda-developers.com/how-to-use-windows-11/

Cohen, J. (2021, October 26). *The best Windows 11 tips and tricks.* PCMAG. https://www.pcmag.com/how-to/best-windows-11-tips-and-tricks

Computer Hope. (n.d.). *Windows 11 Help and Support.* Www.computerhope.com. Retrieved March 10, 2022, from https://www.computerhope.com/windows-11.htm

Fedewa, J. (2022, February 15). *How to install Android Apps on Windows 11.* How-to Geek. https://www.howtogeek.com/764014/how-to-install-android-apps-on-windows-11/

Fernandez, K. (2021, December 4). *The ultimate guide to Windows 11's touchpad gestures.* MUO. https://www.makeuseof.com/windows-11-touchpad-gesture-guide/

Gewirtz, D. (n.d.). *6 ways to customize Windows 11.* ZDNet. Retrieved March 10, 2022, from https://www.zdnet.com/paid-content/article/6-ways-to-customize-windows-11/

Gralla, P. (2021, December 14). *Windows 11 cheat sheet.* Computerworld. https://www.computerworld.com/article/3644474/windows-11-cheat-sheet.html

GuruMandadi@TWC. (2021, October 3). *How to use the new Photos app in Windows 11.* The Windows Club. https://www.thewindowsclub.com/how-to-use-the-new-photos-app-in-windows-11

Hachman, M. (2022a, February 1). *Forget Outlook: Why Windows Mail is one of the best email apps.* PCWorld. https://www.pcworld.com/article/606623/the-best-email-client-for-you-may-be-mail-not-outlook.html

Hachman, M. (2022b, February 17). *Windows 11's windowed gaming and HDR are about to get a lot better.* PCWorld. https://www.pcworld.com/article/615360/new-windows-11-build-reveals-new-pc-gaming-hdr-improvements.html

Hoffman, C. (2021, June 25). *What's the difference between Windows 10 and Windows 11?* How-to Geek. https://www.howtogeek.com/737186/whats-the-difference-between-windows-10-and-windows-11/

Huculak, M. (2021a, October 5). All the ways to open Settings on Windows 11. Windows Central. https://www.windowscentral.com/how-open-settings-app-windows-11

Huculak, M. (2021b, October 5). Here's what's new with the Windows 11 File Explorer. Windows Central. https://www.windowscentral.com/whats-new-file-explorer-windows-11

Huculak, M. (2021c, October 11). How to be more productive using Desktops on Windows 11. Windows Central. https://www.windowscentral.com/how-be-more-productive-using-desktops-windows-11

Huculak, M. (2021d, November 22). All the tips to personalize your Windows 11 desktop. Windows Central. https://www.windowscentral.com/how-change-look-and-feel-windows-11

James, D. (2021, October 13). Optimize Windows 11 for gaming. PC Gamer. https://www.pcgamer.com/windows-11-gaming-optimization/

Kelly, B. (2021, November 1). Microsoft Teams will be native in Windows 11 operating system. Www.nojitter.com. https://www.nojitter.com/team-collaboration-tools-workspaces/microsoft-teams-will-be-native-windows-11-operating-system

Kumar, R. (2022a, January 4). How to use the Windows 11 Calendar app. All Things How. https://allthings.how/how-to-use-the-windows-11-calendar-app/

Kumar, R. (2022b, January 17). How to Use Microsoft To Do on Windows 11. All Things How. https://allthings.how/how-to-use-microsoft-to-do-on-windows-11/

Merriman, C. (2022, January 3). How to boot Windows 11 in Safe Mode. IT PRO. https://www.itpro.co.uk/operating-systems/microsoft-windows/361662/how-to-boot-windows-11-in-safe-mode

Microsoft. (2002, January 6). Microsoft windows xp sales exceed 17 million copies just over two months after worldwide debut. Microsoft Stories. https://news.microsoft.com/2002/01/06/microsoft-windows-xp-sales-exceed-17-million-copies-just-over-two-months-after-worldwide-debut/#:~:text=Gift%20Ideas-

Muchmore, M. (2022, January 19). The Best New Features in Windows 11's Photos App. PCMAG. https://www.pcmag.com/news/best-new-feautures-in-windows-11s-photos-app

Neagu, C. (2021, September 13). How to start Windows 11 in Safe Mode (8 ways). Digital Citizen. https://www.digitalcitizen.life/windows-11-safe-mode/

Paruthi, N. (2021, November 13). How to use the Windows 11 Photos app. MUO. https://www.makeuseof.com/how-to-use-the-windows-11-photos-app/

Patkar, M. (2017, November 28). The easy guide to Google Chrome. MUO. https://www.makeuseof.com/tag/browsing-at-warp-speed-your-guide-to-chrome/

Pidgeon, E. (2017, October 16). Windows 10 Tip: Get started with the Windows 10 Maps app. Windows Experience Blog. https://blogs.windows.com/windowsexperience/2017/10/16/windows-10-tip-get-started-windows-10-maps-app/

Rayome, A. D. (2022a, February 16). Windows 11 vs. Windows 10: What's different in Microsoft's new OS. CNET. https://www.cnet.com/tech/computing/windows-11-vs-windows-10/

Rayome, A. D. (2022b, February 17). Get more out of Windows 11 with these 9 hidden features. CNET. https://www.cnet.com/tech/services-and-software/get-more-out-of-windows-11-with-these-9-hidden-features/

Shareef, T. (2021, December 9). The 13 best windows 11 tips and tricks that everybody should know. MUO. https://www.makeuseof.com/windows-11-best-tips-and-tricks/

ShiwangiPeswani@TWC. (2021, October 7). How to use Windows 11 - Tutorial for beginners. The Windows Club. https://www.thewindowsclub.com/windows-11-tutorial-for-beginners

Wawro, A. (2021, November 5). 11 essential Windows 11 shortcuts you need to know. Tom's Guide. https://www.tomsguide.com/news/11-essential-windows-11-shortcuts-you-need-to-know

Whitney, L. (2021, October 25). How to Use the Microsoft Store in Windows 11. PCMAG. https://www.pcmag.com/how-to/how-to-use-the-microsoft-store-in-windows-11

Windsor, G. (2021). How to run project meetings with Microsoft Teams. BrightWork.com. https://www.brightwork.com/blog/microsoft-teams-video-meetings

Made in the USA
Coppell, TX
01 October 2022

83874732R00096